SEASONS OF THE URBAN COYOTE

"COMMUNITY is a word of elastic meaning. It stretches constantly, simultaneously moving in opposite directions: downward, to the individual neighborhood, and outward, to embrace the entire world."

— Paul Ylvisaker, from *An Agile Servant*

"We have braided a sweetgrass community, awakening for each other the knowing that we are not alone. The strength of that community has the power to activate change, and our collective rhizomes are spreading."

—Robin Wall Kimmerer, *Braiding Sweetgrass: Indigenous Wisdom, Scientific Knowledge, And the Teachings of Plants*

"For the time of towns is tolled from the world by funeral chimes, but in nature the universal hours are counted by succeeding tribes of animals and plants, and by growth of joy on joy."

— Ralph Waldo Emerson, "The Poet"

SEASONS OF THE URBAN COYOTE

HOWLINGS ON FAMILY, COMMUNITY
AND THE SEARCH FOR PEACE AND JUSTICE

James P. Lenfestey

NODIN PRESS

9 8 7 6 5 4 3 2 1

ISBN: 978-1-947237-37-7

Library of Congress Control Number: 2021945730

Cover art by Roger Boehm

Published by

Nodin Press
5114 Cedar Lake Road,
Minneapolis, MN 55416
www.nodinpress.com

CONTENTS

SEASON THREE

Preface:
The Maunderings of a Twentieth-Century Man

Dear reader. You hold in your hands the selected maunderings from the past decade or so of a Twentieth Century Man. I was born in the last century, raised in the last century, educated in the last century, and everything I know, understand, or care about was created in the last century, with the exception of the MacBook Air (2008) and the iPhone (2013), necessary survival tools like food, shelter, love, and a Swiss Army Knife.

I love books, bookstores, libraries, liberals, the liberal arts, science, mailed letters and wood fires. I love all facts, few opinions, and Martin Luther King Jr's dream that "the arc of the moral universe... bends toward justice." I love paper and pens, digital printers, email, Google and Wiki. But my brain refuses to accommodate Facebook, Twitter, Instagram, Pinterest, Snapchat, YouTube, Uber, Lyft, WhatsApp, etcetera app infinitum. Apps have their uses, and we who refuse them risk further slippage into the Slough of Irrelevance. But as another Twentieth Century writer, Kurt Vonnegut Jr., used to say, "So it goes."

At 76, I am not helpless. I understand microwave ovens, coffeemakers, refrigerators, gas and electric stoves, dishwashers, and the iPhone (in part), though not leaf blowers and other noisemaking devices. I was an early adopter of the personal computer, purchasing the first portable, an Osborne, the size of a suitcase. It had a five-inch black and white screen operated with primitive Wordstar software. For a writer it was a massive step forward. The "cut" and "paste" commands common today in word processing had been my literal practice. Freelancing at the time, I would type up a draft, then cut it apart and "paste" it back together with scotch tape in better order and photocopy the result. If someone entered my office during this process, the resulting breeze blew paragraphs all over the floor.

My wife Susan, smarter than I, having overheard my screams late into the night over some Wordstar glitch or bug, said she would wait for a personal computer that worked like a car – you get in, turn the key, and drive off. She bought our first MacIntosh. I bought the second, and we have been a Mac family ever since.

But as the new century exploded into new methods for doing old things, my brain decided it has had enough with innovation and would stick to the basics it knew. And so I stand, or sit, or relax, beneath your fingertips like Leonardo's Vitruvian Man, nakedly circumscribed by 20th century limitations, loving best the sound and sense and heft of words pressed on paper.

Susan and I were part of the founding of the *Hill and Lake Press* community newspaper in 1976 and helped celebrate its 40th anniversary in 2016 with a big party. After a 13-year run of monthly columns beginning in 1986, I retired in 1998 to leave space for younger, hungrier voices, and set off on other quests. In 2000, Norton Stillman's Nodin Press published my first book, a selection of those columns, *The Urban Coyote: Howlings on Family, Community and the Search for Peace and Quiet*. Norton kicked it off with a fine celebration at the Woman's Club, complete with cake, and the book trotted out into the known universe until today only a few copies remain on basement shelves. Meanwhile, I published nearly a dozen additional books: seven poetry collections, three anthologies of poetry and essays, and a memoir, *Seeking the Cave: A Pilgrimage to Cold Mountain*, chasing the mysterious source of my love for poetry.

I retired from the StarTribune editorial board in 1998 for the creative writer's path. in 2012 I returned to the practice of monthly columns at the Hill and Lake Press, missing the joy of discovering stories and observations as the world rambled by. The Urban Coyote now sniffs and trots into a 76th year —catholic and curious, local and grandiose, personal and communal, tasting whatever delicious scraps chance uncovers, subject only to the stroking of the sensitive keys of my MacBook Air to shape the story in the hope it pleases the reader as much as it pleased the writer. If you hold this book in your hands, you feel that pleasure, and I thank you.

My MacBook Air gets the last word.

ODE TO MY MACBOOK AIR

I love to get up in the quiet, before the birds
ravage the feeder, open my laptop,
cool to the palms, and let my fingers
soar over the keys like cormorants
over open water, as if free
of care, though in fact
urgent with hunger.

Before I leave for the airy world
I fold the clamshell
back into its quiet life
on the sea floor
where it's blue eye peers out
looking for passing prey,
able to see great distances.

Acknowledgments

I am deeply grateful to the board of directors and editor Jean Deatrick of *The Hill and Lake Press* who allowed me to wander back into regular publication after a minor hiatus of a decade or so in pursuit of other projects. Without them, and the four volunteer neighborhood organizations that support the paper and its home, ours would not be "one of the five best neighborhoods on planet earth."

And to my first and best manuscript readers Miriam Feldman and Thomas R. Smith, who offered clear and hard advice and support in the editing and complicated assembly of this selection, including the decision to keep the order chronological. Thanks to Peter Kramer, architect, furniture designer and publisher of Neo-Functionalist Press, for permission to reprint the four prayers to seasons from his elegant chapbook, FOUR SEASONS. To my wife Susan, a better writer than I plus an adept at 21st century communication forms, who read many of these essays first along the way, offering useful suggestions and fixing countless typos. Gratitude to poet and neighbor Robert Bly for permission to reprint "Gratitude to Old Teachers." Finally, to tirelessly youthful Norton Stillman of Nodin Press, who published the first Urban Coyote collection twenty-two years ago, and eagerly responded yes when I sent him a new column and wondered if he would be interested again. All hail to these book people, my highest praise. Of course any errors, confusions and catastrophes remaining herein are the product solely of my own uncontrollable mind and hideous typing.

SEASON I
PRAYER TO FALL

Who made the colors
hidden beneath green?
Who the umber afternoon?

Where once fluttered
solar-loving shapes
in chlorophyll clothes,
the light dress of summer,
hang husks,
stiff and exhausted,
a rustling chorus
of complaint,
russet, jaune,
dried blood and tan,
crackling skittered
streets and winding ways.

Yet how we love to praise
fall's reverberate hills
crowned with maple fire!
Amazed before oak's
bear paw leaves,
elm's veins, bronzed beech,
aspen's fleece blanket,
a golden-footed path lit
by afternoon slant light.

We with roots in cooler
climes, closer to earth's
white cap than her

fecund, humid belly,
raise our autumn arms
in praise of harvest time,
when work from
dark to dark
will fill our bins.

Then knit barren-fingered limbs
in silent prayer — Dear Gods, allay
our ancient fear diminished light
and heat will disappear.

The Urban Coyote Goes Swimming
(October 2012)

I t is late October. Robert and Ruth Bly's new boulevard maple across Girard Avenue has finally shed its glorious crimson crown. The yellow leaves of our boulevard Norway maples, branches recently trimmed by the Park Board into a semblance of elegance, blanket our yard in a lake of deep yellow. These are the kinds of leaves one stoops to pick up and admire, in disbelief at the intensity of the palette of fall.

The temperature has been rising and falling with the slow breath of change, even in this year of record heat and drought, with evening lows in the twenties forecast for the weekend.

With wife Susan out of town on a generous errand in California with our son and my sister, who is ill, I take the time to bike around the lakes, the kind of activity my now lame knee still allows.

In our busy urban lives, how easy it is to forget the foresight of our forebears—the mothers and fathers of Minneapolis who willed this chain of urban lakes into public, not private hands. They created the most intensively used park system in the state.

My rumbly old bicycle and I rode down Lincoln Avenue toward Kenwood Park through a corridor of golden afternoon light, then along the shore of Lake of the Isles where a few hardy sunbathers soaked up the last seasonal rays on the broad lawn. I passed the construction tangle at the south end of the lake and around the east side of Bde Maka Ska, where a sailing class came about in tight circles like a gyre of white butterflies.

Then around Lake Harriet's forested shore, looking in vain for the eagle said to be resident there. I stopped for conversation with two friends I spotted walking hand-in-hand on the pedestrian path. They inquired of a water bird they had seen, with a long, snakelike neck. Stumped, I later saw it too as I rounded the south end of the lake, a western grebe among the migrating coots and mallards, her long neck swanning in and out of the water. A placid loon idled her singular way in deeper water.

The shores of Harriet and Bde Maka Ska sheltered many more coots and resting gulls, and a remarkable population of human beings—runners, bikers, skaters, roller skiers, photographers, strollers with friends and lovers and children, or those who simply communed with water, our body's ancestral home.

I pulled into the beach at Cedar Lake at Akerberg Point. Alone in fading light, I quickly stripped to my suit and waded into the icy waters. Wind out of the south, the beach was sheltered, the lake a mirror sheen. I waded fast, the only way to deal with brisk water, and at waist high dove once, twice, three times. Emerging like a seal, I noticed a silent kayak floating on the sheer surface. And a quiet fisherman in a canoe stroked silently, the lake otherwise empty, a penny-colored disc inside the colorful frame of forested shore.

My neck began to ache as the blood vessels constricted to save body heat, a sign it was time to head for shore.

A friend in Michigan has developed a rich vocabulary for swimming in northern lakes: "Balmy, Almost Balmy, Nice, Almost Nice, Refreshing, Invigorating, Bracing, Bearable, Cold, Brutal, and Freezing (for which ice must be present)." I deemed today's water temp "bearable," like a cold plunge after a hot sauna.

I returned to the shore, letting the cold water bathe my ailing knee, then turned and plunged two more times. Three times seems necessary, after which the skin glows with radiant appreciation but before the chill gets inside far enough to asphyxiate me.

As I dried off on the darkening shore, the quiet fisherman beached his canoe. He showed me iPhone photos of the five-pound bass he'd caught, then released, and others from other days—tiger muskie, pure muskie, a northern pike half as long as he was. When not working his two jobs, he comes to Cedar Lake. The giant fish he finds with his homemade lures, then releases, give him the tug of another life, as my swims do for me.

I biked home along the bicycle trail to 21st Street, bike light shining, down the hill to Birchbark Books, around Kenwood School and back up Lowry Hill to home.

The gratitude I feel in my entire body for these lakes, preserved for all of us, I can barely say, except to describe one golden late afternoon when a grebe surprised, a fisherman praised his fish, and I plunged three times into the dark well of sweet release.

T'was the Morning of Christmas
(December 2012)

T'was the morning of Christmas, and all through the house on the corner of Girard and Lincoln, chaos was momentarily stilled. A nuthatch and two cardinals, male and female, worked the feeder in the gray light of dawn, the hoggish clan of sparrows apparently too tired from the week of revelry to rise early this day.

Coffee in hand, I reviewed the human affairs of this mid-winter week, and how over the top they are, arguably insane, certainly exhausting, so easy to dispense with, be quiet, read a book, paint a picture, write a poem. And yet how necessary, this holiday located in the heart of midwinter when sunlight reaches its lowest ebb, celebrating light in the pit of darkness. To wit:

Susan, the madwoman of Winter Solstice, prepared the grounds for our annual celebration. Literally. She arranged a ring of trees in our tiny back yard – leftover spruce and balsam fir from her favorite Christmas tree farmer – inside of which she places a fire pit borrowed from a friend. Inside the house, she laced vines and flowers and candles into every opening. Delicious food appeared, also prepared by friends, elegantly presented, fragrant to behold. All of this cold weather activity will raise funds for Beacon, a new non-profit housing collaborative committed to ending urban homelessness, "bringing the warmth and dignity of a home to those who have none."

The benefit crowd that poured in on Winter Solstice Eve limited itself generally to displays of excess slightly below the threshold of indecency. Still, two extraordinary happenings must be remarked.

The backyard solstice fire generated heat and light from 9 p.m. to 1 a.m., during which most of the good poetry of the western world was proclaimed. Memorable this year was Win Rockwell's annual recitation of Robert Service's "The Cremation of Sam McGee," while others added poems by Robert Bly, Mary Oliver, Louise Erdrich and Emily Dickinson, the surprise *piece de resistance* a witty song by Ogden Nash sung by Binky Rockwell, stealing the show. And this. Poet Thomas R. Smith's newest chapbook, "The Night We Saved the Beatles," inspired the throng around the fire to attempt the Beatle's Winter Solstice anthem, "Here Comes the Sun." Despite numerous gaps in lyrics, rhythm, pitch and melody, the overall effect was a soaring choral invitation.

Meanwhile inside the house, a wild dancing had commenced. Among the extraordinary moves busted on the worn oak living room floor, by all accounts the most astonishing were by Hizzoner Mayor Rybak and Her Honor Megan O'Hara dancing Gangnam style! If you don't know what Gagnam style is, you live in planetary darkness, as the Korean dance craze surpassed one billion views on Youtube over Solstice week, as reported by our 16-year-old grandson familiar with such matters. Had Mr. and Mrs. Mayor been videotaped, the remaining six billion would have been hooked, our city's First Couple raised such a joyful romp.

As the light of day followed the longest night, Christmas proclaimed its ancient story. Do you know it? No, not the one about the red-suited man dispensing greedy treasure. The much quieter tale of a newborn babe, and how wise men and wise women moved his actual birthdate to coincide with the Roman celebration of Saturnalia to combine midwinter revels with the birth of a transformative ethic: "Do unto others as you would have them do unto you," echoing the similar sentiment voiced by Confucius and Greek philosophers centuries prior. The Golden Rule has ruled ever since, if honored only in the breach. But it is central this hallowed day of the year which is about others, not ourselves.

So after we cleaned up the exhausted Solstice remnants and placed the recycling into the cavernous interior of the mysterious new blue container and counted the benefit checks, we deeded house and hearts to the visiting next generation, in our case three children with spouses and four of six grandchildren including four-year-old twins, plus one boyfriend and one girlfriend.

Susan warped into her second Fanny and Alexander phase, the rest of us dazzled into action. A tree suddenly appeared and was trimmed with homemade gingerbread cookies decorated by the children, a delicious Christmas Eve dinner was consumed, made by a son and his girlfriend, stockings were hung by the chimney with care by a daughter and her husband, a plate of cookies and carrots for Santa and his reindeer was set by the fireplace, and wine and eggnog and bright-eyed conversation and brighter memories carried through the long Christmas Eve night. Except in the case of Grandpa Coyote, who had quietly slipped off to bed.

So that he could rise up with the cardinals and nuthatches when all is calm, all is bright, and a sense of wild wonder rules the world. The story of the birth of a baby, plus the rising mid-winter sun enveloped in a coat of frosty innocence, allowed him to dream—if only dream—that the gods of joyful fantasy and earthly proportion had returned once more.

Soon enough grandchildren will descend the stairs like nuthatches, twittering with delight, parents following like woozy cardinals, and I'll put away my keyboard for the year 2012. I am certain that the rest of this day will include both pleasure and pain in the form of gifts that please mostly and boiled chestnuts painfully peeled for stuffing, a once hateful task now insisted on by grown children, for pain is tied to memory, as is joy when the sun remembers to return.

Right now, in early morning peace and quiet, I feel, as Yeats once did, that I "am blessed and can bless."

Coyote Walks Out
(March 2013)

March in Minnesota historically comes on like a lion and goes out like a lion, leaving its victims bitten by howling blizzards and covered with shaggy snow. But in our globally warmed world, March moves more like a lion in galoshes, with temperatures randomly above and below freezing, a mix of snow and rain and greasy sidewalks. Still, what a pleasure as the weather turns toward Spring to risk one's life to walk (or trot) through puddles and over black ice to the many destinations new and old easily reachable on foot (or paws) in our neighborhood, a pedestrian paradise.

When Mrs. Coyote and I became empty burrowers several years ago, we took a desultory look at apartments and condos, some with super views and lots of arty happenings. We demurred for many reasons, including the fact that our heart wasn't in it. A major reason is the walkability of our neighborhood.

We can walk to Kowalski's grocery store and the Wedge Co-op, to Walgreens, Anderson Cleaners, Seb Joe's for ice cream and Isles Buns for buns, to Patina for gifts and Birchbark Books and the Uptown Library for books and solace. To Kenwood and Jefferson schools and the Kenwood Rec center for education mental and physical. To the Walker Art Center and sculpture garden and Kenwood park for jogging and sledding and Lake of the Isles for limping (bad knee), skating and skiing, to Cedar Lake for swimming and snowshoeing. The only important destination we can no longer reach with absurd ease is a post office, formerly located inside Burch Pharmacy, now at 10th St between Hennepin and First Avenues, walkable or bikeable on nice days, or choose the friendly UPS Store at 28th and Hennepin.

That leaves only dining out, something that interests this urban Coyote only if he can walk or trot or bike. As a home-based writer, I no longer take breakfast meetings, a staple of Minnesota culture, as mornings are sacred writing time. Instead, I have meetings at lunch. Over the years, some my favorite local lunch destinations have vanished, in the always volatile restaurant business, but many are alive in fact or in memory.

I'll mention only one, my oldest and most consistent flame, Lynn Gordon's French Meadow Bakery and Café on Lyndale Avenue and 26th Street, easy biking or a healthy walk. Organic from birth in 1985, it is sustainable and delicious to the core, and who is not ennobled dining under a quotation from Wendell Berry boldly stenciled on the wall: *"The care of the Earth is our most ancient and most worthy, and after all our most pleasing responsibility. To cherish what remains of it and to foster its renewal is our only hope."* Let us walk there together.

&

A Thousand Swans
(April 2013)

I was having a rocky morning. Up before dawn, I was reading "Coal River," assigned for a book review, the depressing tale of mountaintop mining in Appalachia and its devastating corruption not only of the landscape but of the people and political system there. I needed to suppress that bummer with a run around Lake of the Isles in the fresh morning air.

With questionable knees, I had resumed jogging but only in reasonable weather, so had missed for several weeks as the winter bitterly hung on into April.

This morning, April 13, the air felt a bracing warmth at 31 degrees with a bright southern sun. Snow and ice loitered on the north side of streets as I ran, the legacy of an April Fool's snowstorm, but the sky was clean and clear. At the lake, a pair of Blue-winged teal raced over the icy surface looking in vain for open water. A few early arrival Canada geese hunched in the ice near Cranberry Island patiently awaiting the thaw.

On the west side of the lake I encountered an old friend jogging with his dog, so we stopped at Isles Deli for a latte. Then I stopped next door at Birchbark Book to pick up a book I had ordered.

At Birchbark, manager Susan White was minding everything as always, fresh and enthusiastic even with twelve hours days. I picked up the book, "The Republic of Poetry" by Martin Espada, the brilliant and fun Puerto Rican-American lawyer-professor poet I recently heard read at The Loft Literary Center. As usual, I found myself unable to resist a second book, neighbor Robert Bly's newest set of translations, twenty poems by the Persian poet Hafez, displayed on the counter. Susan generously added to my bag a braid of sweetgrass with its haunting natural fragrance. It was already a better day.

At 9:22 am, book bag in hand, I began the short jog home on the trail along the north side of Lake of the Isles, but stopped cold when I heard a distant, noisy confusion. Looking up, I expected perhaps a vee of migrating Canada Geese, a not uncommon sight and sound here during spring migration season, yet I saw nothing against the clear blue morning sky over a low scrim of distant cloud. Suddenly, out of the southern sun a thousand waterfowl materialized, their vee formations spread horizon to horizon. As the massive birds passed overhead I watched white wings and long white necks strain ahead of powerful white bodies trailing long black legs, all illuminated in golden morning sun. *Cygnus columbianus,* Tundra swans!

I watched and listened as cacophonous skeins one after the other passed north over Kenwood Park traveling toward the potholes of North Dakota and southern Alberta and Manitoba, eventually to settle in breeding grounds along the

Arctic Ocean. They had left their wintering grounds along the Atlantic coast, swept around the southern tip of lake Michigan, to arrive just at the moment I was in the right place and the right frame of mind to be astonished.

Several more massive vees of elegant crossbow bodies noisily clattered overhead all morning as I settled down in my home office to capture the moment on paper before it disappeared over the horizon of memory.

Sometimes grace appears suddenly, out of the blue. Sometimes we are lucky enough to be ready. This morning I was open like a book to what the spring sky offered.

Eagle Over Bde Maka Ska*
(September 2013)

To give myself an excuse to sneak a delicious afternoon latte at Rustica, I booked an appointment next door at Calhoun Vision to cover my tracks. Dr. Granville Lawrence, mad motorcyclist and neighborhood comedian who also happens to be an Eye Doc, has been feeding me jokes and providing me eyeglasses since the Pleistocene. After we discussed the script of his newest unpromising play (in which men who begin as boors end as boors) and handicapped the mayor's race (why are we not running along with everyone else?), he checked my eyes, upped my prescription to a level appropriate to my advanced age, and eased me out the door. After which I happily loitered over the latte next door and read a long, involved article in T*he New Yorker.*

---

*The lake was named Calhoun when I wrote this piece. The Minnesota DNR in 2017 decided to revert to a name given to the lake by the Dakota: Bde Maka Ska, "White Earth Lake."

In a state of informed, caffeinated bliss, I drove home along the south shore of Bde Maka Ska. The late September day was warm as late August, with gusty winds whooshing through the cottonwoods, raising foot tall whitecaps on the lake. Two sailboats heeled to the rails while a brace of colorful windsurfers skittered along the surface in ideal wind conditions. Impulsively I pulled into the parking lot to watch them, walking across the busy pedestrian and bike paths to the shore.

With wind in my hair and sun warming my face, I watched master sailboarders rocket past. The sight reminded me the days when I too was mad for this perfect combination of wind and water, board under my feet, boom straining hands, the more wind the better. For the first time in a decade I regretted giving away my sailboard and gear, antiques now in the face of these racy sails and ever shorter, ever faster boards. Still, a joy to watch them balance gracefully against wind and water. I felt as if I happened upon the America's Cup race or a flock of excited water birds.

Then I looked up. A bald eagle rode the wind not thirty feet above my head, nearly still. I watched transfixed as it navigated the gusts, white tail wide and ruddering, wings steady, wing tip feathers fingering the details of the wind. His head white like mine, his golden beak hooked like my golden nose, his sharp eyes (like mine after I get my new prescription), he scanned the shoreline below. I imagined what he saw from his high angle, without glare off the surface of the water, an open window above unsuspecting fish. As I watched, he slowly lowered his claws, like golden landing gear, then raised them, head sweeping back and forth. He lowered them again and suddenly swooped toward the lake, scooping a bass in his claws. He rose heavily, flapping his broad, dark wings, and wheeled downwind to settle on a cottonwood branch, where he tore into his fresh catch not far from the local fish restaurant where several dozen humans did the same.

I remember when there were no eagles in this city, and few in the Midwest. They had been extirpated by the ravages of the pesticide DDT that bioaccumulated and softened their eggshells, the eggs collapsing under the weight of baffled brooding parents. Because the use of DDT has long been restricted, we can now see eagles windsurfing or dining on fresh fish just like one of the locals. Which now they are.

For those who despair that we humans will never solve the environmental crisis, the recovery of eagles reminds us solutions are within our grasp. President Kennedy read Rachel Carson's story on the effects of DDT in *The New Yorker*, then her book *Silent Spring*, and set his science advisory committee to the task to regulate DDT. He did so despite warnings of dire economic consequences. The opposite turned out to be true.

President Obama faces a similar executive decision this year – denying a permit for the Keystone XL Pipeline to cross the border from Canada to the US. This is in not an easy decision, as friendly neighbor Canada desperately desires an oil outlet to the sea, and it will create construction jobs down the middle of America. But the harsh reality is that this pipeline will allow vastly more of Alberta's viscous tar sands, a "carbon bomb," to detonate in overseas markets, something the Canadians cannot accomplish inside their own country given spirited spiritual opposition by Native nations and many others.

Whatever President Obama chooses, I will continue to support him, as he clearly understands the crisis of climate change as described in the latest United Nation's report released this month, and he has acted vigorously to limit emissions despite seamless Republican oil-fueled opposition. Still, he must ensure that heavy tar sands oil never strike the sea and multiply the frightening carbon burden our children and grandchildren already carry into the future.

Remember Rachel Carson, the courageous scientist who proved, in spite of a chorus of deniers, that DDT crippled bird populations. Then remember President Kennedy, who acted with courage bolstered by that science. So that I can describe today men and women and children and a bald eagle racing together over the shimmering surface of an urban lake in inspiring wind.

> 🕊

The Urban Coyote Stays Warm
(January 2014)

Like all of you, I am hugging tight my natural gas furnace this winter, letting the Arctic "polar vortex" swirl outside the windows like the evil white witch of Narnia. How I praise my humming high-efficiency furnace, and the pipes below the frozen sidewalks that bring natural gas to our houses.

How happy I am also that we super-insulated this old house at the corner of Girard and Lincoln when we moved in 32 years ago, and added energy-efficient materials, including double pane windows, when we remodeled twenty-five years ago. And how I replaced a furnace along the way with the highest efficiency heat pump I could find.

As all the while the price of natural gas continued to fall, due to the fracking revolution that frees gas and oil trapped in shale deposits formerly impossible to recover. All of us in frigid HLP land benefit from this revolution. If only the climate weren't paying the price.

Once coal would have warmed our houses, and if you lived in Green Bay, Wisconsin, my father's trucks would have rattled fist-sized chunks of anthracite down your basement chute for you to shovel into boilers from which fat ducts like arms allowed heat to rise through the house while black cinders and thick soot swirled up the chimney. City air a hundred years ago was dark with feathers of ash and smudges of smoke emerging from every house and factory, a recipe for asthma and worse.

Sometime in the middle of the last century oil became cheaper and easier to transport than coal, so households removed their giant old coal furnaces in favor of smaller oil burners, with oil storage tanks buried in the yard filled by visiting oil trucks. That's how it worked when we moved into the neighborhood in 1974. A Rollins Oil truck pulled into the driveway at 1925 Girard on a regular basis. The driver pushed a ten-foot stick down into our oil tank buried under the driveway to measure the contents, then filled it to the brim. I changed out that oil burner few years later in favor of cheaper, cleaner, more reliable pipeline natural gas.

All that time coal and nuclear and Canadian hydro powered the electricity that flows from my outlets like water from spigots whenever needed. Thank you, utility infrastructure, I praise you every day.

Yet now I fight to close all remaining coal-burning electricity plants, fight the Keystone tar sands pipeline that wants to bring more oil, fight the worst excesses of fracking that brings cheap gas, and plan to change my house fully to solar and wind-powered electricity as soon as possible. What happened?

Our planet caught a fever. The invisible carbon dioxide molecules still spewing from fossil-fueled chimneys radically warm the atmosphere, dangerously acidify the oceans, accelerate extreme weather events, and destabilize the jet stream. Holy Polar Vortex! So it's time to change fuels again.

I will not be the first neighbor to implement solar-powered electricity, but I will be one of the first to do so in a new way, through a subscription to a community solar garden, as our house on the corner of Girard and Lincoln is shaded by boulevard trees.

Community solar gardens, enabled by the Legislature last session (thank you Sen. Dibble, thank you Rep. Hornstein), required utilities to obtain 1.5% of their electricity from solar by 2020. Community solar gardens are allowed to achieve a portion of that. Numerous companies sprouted up to sell households or renters shares in their solar gardens, large photovoltaic arrays efficiently sited on warehouse roofs or brownfield developments or fallow cornfields then tied into the electric grid. The initial investment builds and guarantees the array, insulates the homeowner from rising electricity rates, and ensures that annual usage is provided by the sun, not coal, gas or nuclear.

Were all of this to be condensed into doggeral, it might go like this:

> *Once I loved my heat of coal*
> *and once my pail of oil,*
> *and once my pipe of ancient gas,*
> *but always loved the soil.*
> *And to be fair, also clean air.*
> *And so I walk, I run*
> *to greet the energy of the sun.*

Coal, oil, gas, sun. If you say it that way, it's simply the next logical step.

The Superbowl of Sunshine
(February 2014)

Our two daughters paid us a visit this week from Seattle. Yes, *that* Seattle, the dour, rainy, caffeinated seacoast metroplex that just trounced the Denver Broncos in the Superbowl and turned out three quarters of a million people for the downtown celebration. Go 'Hawks!

Both our daughters, otherwise sensible women, are eager members of the fabled Twelfth Man, the mad fan enthusiasm that has snatched that city from under its perpetual raincloud.

Think of it. Seattle today is one of the major go-to cities on the continent, booming home of grunge and Microsoft and Costco and Starbucks and Amazon and the Fred Hutchinson Cancer Research Center, gaining Fortune 500 companies faster than Minneapolis once did. Seattle is also now bigger than we are, Seattle-Tacoma-Bremerton ranked 13th in the nation with 3.5 million ecstatic Seahawks fans, The Twin Cities metro area with 2.9 million despairing Vikings fans.

Also, Seattle has a new Rock and Roll museum. And a waterfront undergoing striking reclamation, tearing down the waterfront freeway in favor of a multi-billion-dollar tunnel, freeing up views and real estate values the way San Francisco did two decades age when it reclaimed the Embarcadero. Go '49ers.

Meanwhile in Minnesota the Vikings fired one losing coach and hired another amid a blizzard of low expectations, admitting they are sticking with quarterback Christian Ponder another year. Have they no shame? Go Vikings?

But before we allow ascendant Seattlehawks to screech too loudly their superiority, let's consider the rest of the evidence.

In the time we have raised our four children here, the eldest now somewhere north of forty-five, the Minnesota Twins won not one but two World Series. The kids still pull out the old VHS tapes and watch Jack Morris mow 'em down for eleven innings and Kirby Puckett "touch 'em all."

And Minneapolis has already reclaimed our industrial riverfront, now vibrant with bike trails, expensive condominiums and the spectacular Guthrie, beginning with far-sighted Mayor Don Fraser and sidekick Rip Rapson way back in 1980.

And two weeks ago tens of thousands of Minnesotans skied and strolled the Luminaria Loppet on Lake of the Isles, citizens glowing not with football enthusiasm but with winter wonder. Did you see the illuminated polar bear this year?

And as both our daughters make clear, the Minneapolis art scene – the MIA, the Walker, the Weisman and more – is far superior to Seattle's. Case in point. I attended a lecture last week at the MIA by Maxwell Hearn, curator of the Chinese galleries at the Metropolitan Museum of Art in New York. He stated, clearly and for the record, that after the Met with its 50 rooms of Chinese Art, the MIA has the best Chinese art collection in the country.

You know the rest of the litany of Twin Cities superlatives: The second most Fortune 500 companies per capita (after Connecticut, next to New York City so it doesn't count, we're next to Fargo), the most literate population in the nation (we are practically Canadian!), the most and best live theater per capita, consistently the smartest K-12 students versus other states (vying with Massachusetts), and a population with the second longest life expectancy in the nation (after Hawaii, which also doesn't count). And public radio, our daughters exclaim, don't forget Minnesota Public Radio, so good here, so lame in Seattle!

And whenever I want to put an exclamation point on the fundamental superiority of Minneapolis, I cite this telling stat: an average of 196 sunny and partly sunny days a year, versus 58 sunny days in Seattle, 155 rainy ones!

Today, as our eldest daughter prepares to fly back to Seattle to rejoin her growing, moldy brood, she and my wife sit in our kitchen, the outside temperature a sparkling zero degrees F, inside temperature warm and bright, sunlight radiating through south-facing double pane windows like a hearth fire. We bask at our sunny solar-heated windows like seals.

OK, Seattle has Mt. Rainer, Minneapolis the Polar Vortex. But only rarely can one actually see Mt. Rainer as it is commonly buried in a constant scrim of hissing clouds. We Minnesotans not only get to see the glorious white quilt of winter shining around us under blue skies, but get to feel it too. The sun warms not only our backs and faces but our spirits as it rises ever higher in the sky, higher than Mt. Rainer on a clear day, higher even than the screech of the soaring Seattle Seahawks.

Abundant sunlight is Minnesota's 12th Man against Seattle, the advancing Bigfoot of the Pacific Northwest, where the hoodie sweatshirt is a fashion statement because you *need* one every day against the misty inclemency. Now if the Vikings could only draft the next Russell Wilson at quarterback!

It All Started with WESAC
(March 2014)

MY wife and I are about to take off to New Mexico for the state basketball tournament. Our grandson's team is seeded 5th, the highest ever for his school. The team is undefeated in the conference. And our grandson, captain for three years, is not only very good, he loves the competition.

For which I am grateful to two factors. First, the athletic gene bought to the family from our son's wife, whose brother was a number one draft choice in hockey by the New York Rangers, out of Brown University no less. The King family's got game, and the Lenfestey family now gets the credit.

The second is WESAC, that strange acronym for West Side Athletic Club that we first encountered on kids' t-shirts when we moved here in 1974. Our eldest son, the father of that basketball star, was entering second grade at Kenwood School. One day as I was jogging around Lake of the Isles I saw children playing soccer on a field at the far south end. I stopped to watch, and met Dan Shulman. Turns out he was a founding coach of WESAC soccer, a new sport in the neighborhood. Soon enough I was talked into "coaching" the youngest WESAC bairns as they ran all over the field like a herd of monkeys. I knew nothing about soccer but no such knowledge apparently was required back then. More like a police function. Keep the kids out of the street and following the ball like lemmings.

Sixteen years later that son was goalie on his school's soccer team that twice competed in the finals of the state tournament, losing on the coldest day ever for a soccer game at the Blaine playfields, a bitter icy wind whipping out of the north, we parents well remember. Like this winter. And now his son is a basketball star.

Somewhere along the way I mastered the acronym WE-SAC and went on to coach boy's and girls' basketball teams, rising on the Peter Principle into the vacuum of League Coordinator, ordering t-shirts, scheduling gym time, all the stuff the park board staff mercifully does now.

Our two sons and later our daughter loved both soccer and basketball, our second son already plotting the great moves he will instill in his son Isaac as soon as he turns four months old.

Oddly, I was never – how shall I put this – "talented" as a basketball player, never mind soccer, having scored but two points my entire freshman season for the DePere, Wisconsin Redbirds, the stands erupting when the skinny kid threw up a desperate two-hander that miraculously banked through.

Now my wife and I jet over the snow caps of the Sangre de Christo Mountains into winter weather warm and dry with cobalt blue skies abounding overhead. To spend the day inside a sweaty gymnasium with hundreds of screaming high school students and parents and grandparents urging teams to victory in the joy of competition.

This final game of the regular season was tied 70-70 in regulation, heading into overtime, when I observed our grandson laughing and chatting with the coach of the opposing team. I later found out what he was saying at that tense moment. "Isn't this fun!"

How I Spent the First Day of Spring
(April 2014)

I am not a member of any organized political party. I'm a Democrat. – Will Rogers.

After the near record snowfall on the heels of April Fool's Day, melting rivulets and soaring birdsong raised a mighty chorus on Sunday, April 6th. Spring had finally arrived, the mercury rising to an ecstatic 65 degrees. What an opportunity to spend a glorious day communing outdoors with intimations of fecundity.

My joy was muted, therefore, upon entering the dim recesses of Ramsey Jr. High School at 1pm for the Hennepin County DFL convention, to which I was an alternate delegate supporting candidate Marion Greene for County Board, our former state legislator. The main event was endorsement of one of four candidates to replace District Three commissioner Gail Dorfman, who had stepped down, requiring a special election. All the delgates understood that "no endorsement" was certain and that the candidates would move quickly on to the special primary election on April 29, but the ritual of fruitless communal gatherings is a tradition of Democrats, so I felt compelled to participate.

When I saw the long line of fellow delegates disappearing down the entrance hall corridor like a herd of scruffy sheep, my feelings grew even more mixed. Democracy in action! DFL disorganization! Glorious spring day!

The line inched imperceptibly toward a distant credentialing table. Passing the time, I high-fived friends and acquaintances wearing Marion's green t-shirts and slapping

Greene stickers on the shirts of others. I had a leisurely conversation with a friend I hadn't seen in years. He sported the yellow t-shirt of Greene's opponent, his neighbor. We reminisced about the deaths of our mothers and how we missed our kids now scattered around the globe.

Meanwhile, the convention failed to start at 1:30pm as advertised, the registration process dragging into midafternoon, delegates slowly receiving orange tags, pink for alternates. We finally assembled in the auditorium and the convention Chair gaveled the convention to order by pounding his palm on the table.

The first item of business was the unopposed endorsement of Hennepin County Attorney Mike Freeman, endorsement quickly granted, in gratitude for which he recited some impressive accomplishments, including violent crime down 40% in the county last year and excellent new programs to divert small time drug users to treatment and snatch truant children back to school. Including applause, the process took five minutes, right according to schedule.

The second routine item was the election of Hennepin County DFL officers and steering committee. The nominating committee reported that exactly 19 people had volunteered for the 19 slots. Perfect. No contest, so a call for unanimous ballot was in order, then on to the main event.

That logical trajectory was nipped in the bud when someone spontaneously rose from the audience to nominate a second person for chair, to a chorus of groans. That random act required the existing nominee to make her allotted one-minute speech, saying she hoped to help the party be better organized. The new second nominee was not in attendance. Rather than provoke a lengthy vote, the first nominee withdrew her name, leaving again but one candidate for the position. Done deal.

If only. A flurry followed of amendments, points of order, points of personal privilege, charges and countercharges, as people lined up on both sides of the microphone like an Iraqi election. If the nominee were not here, how did we know she wanted the job? Was not attendance required? Why had she not been vetted by the nominating committee? Gender? The by-laws state the vice-chair must be the opposite gender of the chair. Point of clarification: Not the "opposite gender," just "not the gender" of the chair nominee. More clarifications, obfuscations, head scratching procedural impediments. We finally voted to require the non-attending nominee to submit a letter ex-post facto. But is she really an organized person? We don't know, but the nominee, who withdrew, clearly was not, given what happened next.

The main event finally at hand, all four candidates poised their troops to wave signs and try to persuade uncommitted delegates to cross the Rubicon.

But wait. The Chair announced there were ongoing problems with credentials. No one had thought to bring maps of the district, and some delegates were apparently seated in the wrong precincts.

Fortunately a calm Senator Scott Dibble rose to settle the question. He reported he had talked to the four campaigns, and none was comfortable with the credentialing debacle unfolded around us. All agreed there should be a vote for no endorsement, we adjourn, and the candidates proceed to campaigning for the special primary election on April 29, the two winners moving to the special election on May 13.

Stunned silence greeted the clear good sense of Scott's proposal. But these are DFLers. Two lines again formed at the microphone, with fiery speeches in favor and opposed to the proposal. The most heated noted that they had already sacrificed most of the first glorious day of spring to the dark adolescent halls of Ramsey Jr. High, and now for nothing???? Others noted, a bit more soberly, that indeed the credentials hanging around their necks were unrelated to the precinct where they actually lived.

In the end Senator Dibble's sensible resolution prevailed by a large majority of delegates, real and imposters, and we finally adjourned. As frustrated, exhausted, and unfulfilled delegates rushed for the exits, the chair reminded us of our sacred duty to clean up after ourselves. I am proud to report the auditorium ended the day spotless. After which delegates and alternates stumbled out into the blinding light of a glorious late afternoon sunset to arrive home just in time for "60 Minutes."

Some random benefits accrued from sitting for four hours in very hard auditorium chairs to accomplish nothing. For example, I had a long talk with Larry Gibson, retired marketing exec at General Mills. We agreed he was the oldest delegate in attendance at 85, until he remembered that his wife Lois is 86. They have attended DFL conventions since 1968, the year Senator Eugene McCarthy ran against incumbent Democrat President Lyndon Johnson over the war in Vietnam and permanently enshrined chaos as a feature of Democratic conventions. Will Rogers was right.

But here's the thing. All that chaos has rolled a reluctant country relentlessly forward, on civil rights, women's rights, gay rights, disability rights, education, economic opportunity, environmental responsibility, green energy and fiscal responsibility, creating a forward-looking state that clobbers our Republican-dominated neighbors in every index of the responsible life, including business environment, employment, educational attainment and support of the arts and the environment. We welcome, care for and inspire everyone, of whatever race, gender and political proclivity, who is willing to endure our winters and the chaos of our democracy.

Huzzah for Will Rogers' party. And don't forget to vote in the special primary on April 29 and election May 13. If

I can fritter away the first delicious afternoon of spring for you, you can spend 20 minutes making an informed greene decision.

❧

Remembering Trees Named Celia and Bill
(May 2014)

I stopped at Lake of the Isles recently to admire a pair of visiting loons and was thrilled to discover fox sparrows and a ruby-crowned kinglet desporting in the willow thatch along the shore. And that reminded me of Celia Logan.

When we moved to the neighborhood in 1974, Lake of the Isles was a manicured English park, the grass mown and trimmed right to the water's edge, a lovely promenade. But not good for the lake's water quality, wildlife, or – in the end – us, as few knew then, certainly not me. But Celia did.

Celia lived alone in an apartment on Emerson and Lincoln. She walked the neighborhood daily in a cotton housedress and sturdy brown oxfords, silver hair pulled into a no-nonsense bun, sharp eyes observing the world through bottle-thick glasses.

A deeply knowledgeable naturalist, Celia had initiated a quiet campaign to stop the Park Board from mowing the lake's edge, instead allowing natural vegetation to grow, creating habitat for wildlife while consuming excess phosphorus that otherwise fed annoying algae blooms (this was well before the invasion of the escaped aquarium plant Eurasian water milfoil which creates today's foul mats of vegetation).

She also volunteered as the Dutch Elm Disease monitor for the neighborhood, walking the blocks weekly, head cocked upward, scanning elms for telltale flagging yellow branches that indicated the contagion. That's how she met our family, our heads down in our yard tending a garden of tumbling children, she passing by on her Godly rounds. .

Along the way we coaxed out her biography. She was a mathematics graduate of the University of Minnesota, the only woman in the department. Told women could not do that kind of work, she proved them wrong, spending her entire career in research jobs at Honeywell, again the first and usually only woman in her departments. Although she would never say it, she was a pioneer.

After Honeywell retirement, Celia became our neighborhood's volunteer urban environmentalist, guarding our elms and lakes from foreign invaders and our own ignorance. To honor Celia's service to the neighborhood, we crowned her Queen of Lowry Hill at the very first Lowry Hill festival. I paraded her around the neighborhood in the back of my Chevvy Luv pickup, Susan's woven willow laurel crown on her head, and we planted a hackberry sapling in her honor – a species she recommended – in the new neighborhood park at the corner of Emerson and Franklin.

Today the Celia Logan Hackberry towers stout and strong, filled with leaves of gratitude. Meanwhile, a Google search revealed that Celia M. Logan passed on quietly in 1996 at eighty-nine – no obituary, no plot, no stone, no muss, no fuss.

Reading that, my wife and I decided to visit her tree for an ad hoc memorial. Our arrival at the pocket park at Emerson and Franklin reminded us of a second memorial tree, this one for Bill Smith.

Like Celia, Bill Smith was a solitary. Unlike Celia he was a recluse in his tiny retirement apartment in The Gables on Franklin and Emerson. A farm laborer his whole life, he walked once or twice a week to gather supplies at the local grocery store (now extinct) and to take the air. We got to know Bill slightly because our friend Roger Boehm, the first artist for the Hill and Lake Press, also lived in The Gables, as did our son's best friend Dwyer Reilly with his feisty single mother Colleen. I have a picture of Bill in my mind – slight frame, pale skin, jeans, wire-rimmed glasses, some sort of cap. According to Roger, those were the only clothes he owned. In summer he unstitched the sleeves from his single shirt. In winter he stitched them back on. My wife remembers him trimming the boulevard grass with scissors. He looked up at her with a shy smile as she passed. He could not stop being useful.

On one of his slow outings to the grocery store, Bill was struck by a car and killed in the intersection of Dupont and Franklin, the reason there is a stoplight at that intersection today. Bill had no known relatives, so Roger claimed the box of his ashes and suggested we plant a tree in his memory in the new park across the street. Unknow to me, Roger then drove to the country, returning with a five-foot spruce he had dug up by the roots. Meanwhile, I had purchased a nursery tree. In a sunset ceremony, the Friends of Bill planted the two trees in the new park, Bill's ashes scattered beneath them both.

Today the Bill Smith tree* stands on the side of the hill overlooking Emerson, thick and strong. The spruce grew so rambunctious it overran the sidewalk so was recently replaced by new plantings – shrubs, daffodils and tulips. Unassuming Bill would be fine with that. Wouldn't say a word. Neither would Celia, the Queen of Lowry Hill. So I get to say something here by remembering them both.

---

* A pint of Sebastian Joe's ice cream to the first person who identifies the species of the Bill Smith Tree. I forgot the name, but not the people who inspired it.

Best Tree Identifier Identified

(June 2014)

Last month I asked the help of readers in identifying a tree friends had planted over thirty years ago to honor Lowry Hill resident Bill Smith, struck by a car and killed at the corner of Franklin and Dupont. I offered a pint of Sebastian Joe's ice cream to the first person that gave the correct answer and help me remember what we had once done.

I am happy to report that the winner is Saheli Patel, a fifth grader at Kenwood School. She marched up to the tree with me and confidently identified it. She was so smart and charming and well informed about trees that I asked her to write up her story. The result is printed below, word for word. I attempted to delete the last paragraph as needlessly complimentary to a mysterious "distinguished gentleman" in "traveling kind of shorts." But Saheli's Mom Angie said cutting it would be "a deal breaker." So it remains.

Regards, U. Coyote.

Dear. Mr. Lenfestey –

Thank you for taking me out to ice cream and giving me the chance to be in the paper. This is the story of how I won the contest.

I heard about your tree identification contest from my mom who read it in the Hill and Lakes Press. My mom came home and announced that I could go win a pint of Sebastian Joe's ice cream if I was the first to figure out what an unidentified tree was. I was so excited, I immediately started bugging her with, "when are we gonna go, where is it and do you know anything about the tree already?" She told me that she only knew the location and I had to do the rest of the figuring out because my mom does not know much about trees unless they are fruit bearing trees. She is growing five apple trees as well as a plum, pear, cherry and a lemon tree in our yard but she can't identify other trees unless they are obvious.

My mom took me to a semi-circle with flowers and mulch and at the top was a large 30-40 foot tall tree with slightly heart-shaped, simple, serrated leaves with a uniform leaf base. Right away, just from looking far away, I could tell it was a Little Leaf Linden. I knew this because our neighbors have a tree like this overhanging into our backyard, which is okay. I had identified the tree last fall.

My mom knew I'd be able to identify the tree because of my experience identifying leaves for The Leaf Project at Kenwood School. The Leaf Project was assigned last fall for the fifth-grade class with our teacher Mr. Darwin Lee. We went to Kenwood Park to pick up leaves and then our teacher helped us figure out how to identify a leaf. We picked leaves from other Native trees in the neighborhood. The main components of a leaf are whether or not it is serrated, if it is compound, simple or doubly compound and whether it is lobed, unlobed, alternate or opposite. The project involved collecting leaves (some students collected 30 leaves) and cataloging the leaves and doing observational drawings. We learned about deciduous and coniferous trees. Before this project I knew just about nothing about trees.

Mr. Lee is a very fun and nature loving unique teacher. He tells us many interesting and inspiring stories and reads us books aloud. His assignments are always fun and not boring and he cares about each individual kid.

Thank you again for the ice cream. This was especially nice of you because you no longer eat dessert. You are a very nice man. My mother says you are a distinguished gentleman and I also noticed that you look like a traveler in an old-fashioned book because of your white-pocketed shirt, spectacles, beard and traveling kind of shorts.

Yours sincerely,
Saheli Patel

❧

Wasn't That a Mighty Storm
(July 2014)

June rain clouds sat over the state like a vengeful Louisiana dumping its right-wing swamps upon us. Lake of The Isles overflowed its banks, flooding the walking trail in places and sending mating turtles scurrying for higher ground. Cedar Lake grew deeper, but that could be because so many roasted children bobbed and frolicked in the already warm and weedy water. Good news, our well-built northern sewer system held up, though more than a few basements flooded and famers from Rainy Lake to the Iowa border fished in their fields. An old spiritual popped into my mind:

> *Wasn't that a mighty storm?*
> *Wasn't that a might storm, Lord.*
> *Wasn't that a might storm?*
> *It blew the people all away.*

That song describing Noah's Fludde should be the anthem for the Minnesota summer of 2014.

First, some good news. Friends visiting Minnehaha Falls to admire the enormous volume of whitewater plummeting over the precipice, reported gasping with disbelief along with other onlookers as a kayak suddenly plunged over the lip and disappeared upside down in the boiling foam! The kayaker popped up bloody but unbowed, arms and paddle raised in triumph, issuing a barbaric yawp!

Now the bad news. Swatches of rot appeared in the fence surrounding our lot at the corner of Girard and Lincoln. Meaning I had to buy cans of plastic wood to fill and paint over the wounds.

Which led to good news. As I filled cracks and painted, several neighbors stopped by on their walks, each "cleverly" suggesting I was pulling a Tom Sawyer. Apparently not, as I failed to lure any of them to join me with a brush. Then neighbor Jim McCarthy passed by. A downtown attorney with Jesuit training and Dudley Riggs humor, he handed me a flyer for an Open Eye Puppet Theater performance to take place in his driveway that very evening only a few blocks away.

The rain held off and I joined an audience of children and adults splitting our sides from the punnishing hilarity of "The Magic Boot." At the conclusion, Jim passed a capacious hat and we filled it generously to keep the creative geniuses of Open Eye in our lives.

Then, more bad news. On July seventh the Big One hit, a truly Mighty Storm. Susan and I were in flight from a family wedding in Colorado to MSP, where we planned to rendezvous with our 16-year-old granddaughter and her friend flying in to visit from New Mexico. But we could see out the plane windows a towering angry wall cloud swirling over MSP airport. Where it glowered. And glowered. And sat. Our pilot flew circles over Sioux Falls until local cattle complained of dizziness. Finally he landed in Rochester to refuel and wait out the storm, which soon surrounded Rochester like an invading Cossack army. When the horizontal line squall hit the plane on the tarmac it almost lifted off.

Meanwhile our granddaughter's plane from Albuquerque had also been diverted to Rochester, except it "broke" something on the tarmac waiting in the refueling queue, so our granddaughter, her friend and the other passengers were shuttled to MSP by bus. Meanwhile our flight finally took off for MSP, somehow losing to our luggage.

Good news, we found the girls at MSP in high spirits after the bus ride, albeit tired of mango chips and Cliff bars, and took them home. Bad news, I am typing this column sitting on the floor of MSP baggage claim at 2AM while beleaguered staff sort through thousands of bags, thirty or forty angry displaced travelers ahead of me on the list, other planes having been diverted as far as Madison.

Further inconveniences ensued (have I mentioned the flu?), but none of the people we love were blown away in the Mighty Storm of July, 2014. And our luggage was found, so I rolled in at dawn to tell the tale.

The Mice of Summer
(August 2014)

We north country people love our summer cabins. We love the lake out the porch door shimmering with sun, wind puffs writing their cryptic language across the surface. Fish loiter below waiting to be caught for dinner, or in the case of sturgeon, hang along the bottom waiting for the human era to pass away. White pines sough overhead, their strong black arms reaching over the shore, feathery needles fingering the breeze. Ahh, the cabin.

So who would mind sharing such bounty with a small family of mice? We didn't. During July dinners we would barely startle as they traversed their evening highway between the restaurant below the stove and the wet bar below the sink.

Lately, however, they have grown a bit too comfortable. We began to get the impression we were intruding into *their* kitchen.

One night we returned from a stroll admiring the constellations – The Big Dipper, Orion, The Mighty Mouse – after a delicious homemade dinner. Back in the kitchen we found a house mouse on the counter brazenly munching the heel of our last loaf of bread. A bridge too far.

A trip to the tiny local hardware store offered two trap options. One was the familiar old-fashioned snap trap, a wooden rectangle with a spring and copper trigger on which you cement cheese and risk several digits as you arm the sensitive device. The other was a new-fangled plastic receptacle with a trap door inside of which you place peanut butter (recommended), on the humane theory that the mouse enters and the trap door swings up behind it, then someone releases the mouse into the wild. Hmmm.

I decided to try both and baited up – peanut butter in the plastic contraption, leftover stale shredded cheese onto the snap trap. Results the next morning: Zero for two. Nothing inside the trap door, and the cheese was eaten off the snap trap without springing it.

A Wisconsin boy, I suspected the problem – cheap cheese. The next night I offered tiny wedges of two-year-old aged cheddar from Steve's Cheese, my home town creamery in Wisconsin, ambrosia for a last meal.

That night I baited four snap traps with Steve's and left the failed peanut butter in the plastic trap, but placed it against the farthest, dimmest wall in the pantry. Results the next morning: Six to zero! That's right, six mice in one night! Each snap trap held a rodent bug-eyed with astonishment, while two others milled around inside the plastic gizmo. I thought, I deserve a belt buckle proclaiming "Six in one night!" (If you miss the reference, consult Grimm's fairy tales, "Seven at One Blow.")

A committed recycler, I emptied the bug-eyed bodies onto rocks behind our house to feed the crows. But what to do with the two milling mice foolishly attracted to a patch of Skippy's? I walked them deep into the dark wood, crossing the gravel back road, and launched them onto the forest floor. They could never find the way back from the wilderness, right?

Wrong. The next night I caught one more. Then three more. Then one more. And one more. Eleven with no end in sight.

Still, the traffic noise from the kitchen floor had reduced substantially. No more thundering little feet disrupting the salad course. All is well in the kingdom of the summer cabin. Mostly.

Today I discovered an earwig in the kitchen sink! An *earwig*! That most despicable of insects, with pincers at its mouthparts where you would expect them and at its tail where you would not! The insect that crawls into your ear from under your wig and eats your brains! Or so the folktale says. That battle awaits another day.

Free-Roaming Cats: Unlove Them!
(October 2014)

Let me tell you about the birds and the bees,
and the cats beneath the trees.
Cats killing birds in droves,
and a thing called Unlove!

That's a loose paraphrase of the famous Jewel Akins song from the mid-Sixties. I needed a soft opening for a sensitive topic about a troublesome neighborhood menace. It's time we discussed the facts of life and death about outdoor cats.

According to the American Bird Conservancy:

BULLETIN: "In the U.S., free-roaming domestic cats kill an estimated 1.4-3.7 billion birds and 6.9-20.7 billion mammals. The sheer quantity of cat-caused mortality is staggering. For perspective, consider that 1.4 billion is equivalent to the entire human population of China, the most populous country in the world. As the number of cats continues to grow and owners continue to allow their pets to roam, harmful impacts will surely increase."

BULLETIN: "Domestic cats (*Felis catus*) can provide excellent companionship and make wonderful pets. But when allowed to roam outdoors, this non-native, invasive species threatens the welfare of birds and other wildlife and endangers the integrity of the ecosystems into which domestic cats are introduced."

BULLETIN: "Cats have contributed to the extinction of 33 species across the world and continue to adversely impact a wide variety of species, including those that are threatened or endangered. The ecological dangers are so critical that the International Union for the Conservation of Nature (IUCN) now lists domestic cats as one of the world's worst non-native invasive species."

BULLETIN: What Are Government Scientists Saying About Roaming Cats? "Well-fed cats continue to kill birds. The number of pet cats in the U.S. has increased threefold in the last 40 years and approximately 65% of these are roaming for some portion of the day. These free roaming cats, added to the number of feral cats, total an estimated 140 million cats, which kill on average at least 1.4 million birds per day. In some areas, cat predation has decimated local bird populations, and has led to the disappearance of some species."

A recent report by Smithsonian scientists and the U.S. Fish

and Wildlife Service found that cats kill an estimated 2.4 billion birds each year, underscoring the need for effective solutions to protect wild birds and cats alike."

My presentation of these unadorned cat facts is prompted by the regular appearance in our back yard of not one but two outdoor cats, one jet black, the other calico. Both loiter under our bird feeder, which my wife devotedly stocks with feed priced high as sirloin steak to attract and care for our native feathered friends who flit in three dimensions like human souls. We love them, the cardinals, house finches, goldfinches, nuthatches, chickadees, woodpeckers and numerous glorious passing warblers and orioles in spring and fall.

But these native birds did not evolve with feline predators and so are not wary enough around them on the ground. The cats know this, and catch them, often just for play, sometimes eating them, almost always killing them.

Except, it seems, the English sparrows, an invasive species from Europe, the pigs at the feeder trough. They apparently did evolve with cats as they never seem to get caught by them, instead driving us crazy with their endless proliferation. They are almost as bad as that other import mostly from Europe, *Homo sapiens sapiens*," although "sapiens" said even once – intelligent, thoughtful – is as much up for debate these days as is *felix catus,* both of us ecological menaces as the Arctic collapses above us and songbirds disappear around us.

Please keep your cats indoors. I will thank you. My wife will thank you. And our native birds with thank you with a chorus of song upon their safe return next spring.

Giving Thanks for Our
"Open, Affirming" Neighborhood
(November 2014)

In the aftermath of the nationally stupid midterm elections, in which numerous science-denying, gay-bashing Republicans ascended their ignorant thrones, isn't it just plain wonderful to live in a neighborhood and city where all that nonsense isn't tolerated, one that has left needless hostility behind for the joys and benefits of living together in community?

It was not always thus. When we moved to Minneapolis in 1974, "gay-bashing" was not unknown, including the awful murder of a young gay man in Loring Park, the state's first openly gay hometown.

As a candidate for City Council in 1979 for the seventh ward, which includes Loring Park, I was one of the first public officials, elected or wannabe, to attend the Gay Pride parade, a tradition that had just begun. My visit there was encouraged by gay activists Robert Halfhill and Tim Campbell, the latter the founding editor of our first gay newspaper, The GLC-Voice. They knew I needed the help because the Council district election that year was a three-party race, the first and only time the gay community created its own political party, the Gay Survival Fund, to run a candidate in the Seventh Ward. Campbell's paper impishly endorsed me for mayor over Don Fraser – of course I wasn't running for mayor! I lost the election by a couple hundred votes, the gay party candidate garnering around four hundred. With the split vote, the Republican incumbent won. A good person, hardly a homophobe, she represented us well during her next term. But the election that year threw open the political closet door for gay citizens that would not be closed again.

My wife grew up in a suburb of Chicago that once spent a lot of hidden energy walling out Jews and people of color, until her parents helped break those red lines by inviting in both groups. Those hidden walls fell fast in the early Sixties in historical terms, still a cross was burned on the lawn of the first Black family to move in. A "Christian" Cross!

My church, Plymouth Congregational, bills itself as an "open and affirming" congregation, one that has supported gay rights for decades and civil rights since its founding, firing its first minister in 1858 for *not* taking a strong enough stand *against* slavery. Today our neighborhood is "open and affirming" as well. How good that feels.

Living here is so much better these days – easier, smoother, warmer, no need to exhibit or suppress all that senseless hostility. The neighborhood, church and city are models for ending intolerance that still plagues the American family.

If only the Republican Party would relax their so-called culture wars, let everyone make their own decisions about their own racial and gendered lives and bodies, it might become a serious party in our town again. Wait, that's a hallucination! The three recently elected Minnesota Republican Congressmen -- Eric Paulson, John Kline and Tom Emmer (a truly mean and ignorant bully, as remembered by those who served with him in the state House)-- want to suppress gay and women's rights and climate science and God knows what other facts that trouble them about their ignorant God's creation.

Never mind all that for now. I am in a happy mood celebrating the efflorescence of our neighborhood, with many gay couples rehabbing houses, strolling the streets, relaxing in the parks, not to mention running our businesses, our architecture and law firms, our medical practices, sending their children to our schools, saving our lives, our community, our souls.

Do we need more openness in our community? Sure. But right now, as winter slowly slips into her white cloak and the sun slides under the horizon for three months of well-deserved rest, let us slip into this season's darkness warm in the beacon of our open and affirming neighborhood, churches and synagogues, city government, homes and hearts.

＊

Gifts from Santa's Doctor Bag
(December 2014)

This Christmas I have been inventorying the medical gifts that Santa bought me over my now seven decades of physically somewhat upright life. And so I want to praise a group rarely sung at this or any time of year: The pharmaceutical and medical technology companies, and the doctors who practice with them. Here are a few drugs and medical repairs I am thankful for this Christmas.

As a boy I fell and jammed a fat rusty nail into the thick part of my palm. A tetanus shot and that was that.

My body's joints seem much less grating due to daily pills of glucosamine sulfate – not FDA approved but anecdotally helpful – believed in by my friends and my own knees and hips.

Decades ago, when our children were small, several developed a circular rash. My wife knew right away not only what it was – ringworm or impetigo – but what to do. A common ointment wiped it right out.

As for my troublesome right knee, its torn meniscus was readily repaired by taciturn Dr. Larson, leaving two barely perceptible scars small as pencil erasers. Dr. Scott Anseth waits in the wings to replace the joint if needed.

Meanwhile, painful bone–on-bone friction in my right knee is mitigated by shots into the knee joint of hyaluronic acid, aka rooster comb, replacing the missing cushion for months at a time, returning me to the tennis court to mow down younger competitors like so many rag dolls.

The mesh patch "tacked" inside my lower abdomen by my pal Dr. Dan Dunn easily repaired the hernia I apparently had my whole life, as my father did before me and my son and grandson do today (who knew hernias were genetic!). For years after that arthroscopic operation, which also left two nearly imperceptible scars, I received emails from lawyers urging me to join a class action suit against the manufacturer of the mesh, some apparently defective. Not mine, and no thanks. I am grateful.

As for my heart, it still seems to pump adequately, but if it did not, Medtronic offers any number of replacement parts. And if I decide to deal with stubbornly high cholesterol, there's a statin for that. But first the MRI scheduled for next week will peek inside to see if there are any deposits that could break loose and stroke my brain. That peek will take ten minutes. I have ten minutes.

My grandfather was a country doctor. I still have the native-made snowshoes he used to tramp up farm roads in winter to assist the sick and deliver the babies. Thanks to Louis Pasteur, he well understood the importance of sanitation. Often he took along his young son, my father, in the horse and sleigh to the houses of the afflicted. My father's job was to kindle the fire and boil the water to sterilize bandages.

My grandfather knew his limits. He always carried vials of little white pills in his doctor's bag, which he handed out for countless ailments. They were sugar pills, AKA placebos. He carried them because he understood people needed comfort in their suffering – the placebo effect – and also because he had nothing more effective to offer. He quietly told my father, "before antibiotics, we had nothing – nothing! – against infection and infectious diseases." Without penicillin, pneumonia might have taken my life several times over.

Let's not forget vaccines, including now for pneumonia [and as I edit this, COVID-19.] The scourge of my youth, polio, has been eradicated in this country. We remember childhood friends crippled, some spending a lifetime with leg braces, in wheelchairs, or in an iron lung. No more.

I had whooping cough as a boy. In fact, both my sisters and I had it at the same time. Our sleepless parents carried us one by one into the shower all night to breathe the steam. We survived, but I don't know how our parents did. Today, pertussis is part of the childhood vaccination program that also covers measles, which we also contracted back then, some faces permanently disfigured with pock marks. Never mind diphtheria, which killed millions, including my wife's grandmother, uncle, and nearly her father at age eleven.

Even the frightening beast of cancer has been partially tamed. Years ago our daughter's second-grade friend at Kenwood School died tragically of childhood leukemia, a form of cancer commonly survivable today.

Meanwhile my son-in-law works night and day to understand the tricky scourges of HIV and malaria and resurgent TB [and now COVID-19] to develop vaccines to tame them. He and his team will succeed.

So this Christmas, even though we are right to worry about Ebola, SARS, MERS, West Nile, resurgent TB, environmental toxins and other serious risks (a coronavirus?), let us praise the Santa Claus bag of medical products and procedures that brought us the gifts that have meant, on average, ever longer, healthier, more productive lives.

I await only the invention of the implantable memory chip, so that when I encounter you, my friends, in the grocery store or Walgreens or Birchbark Books, I will remember your names on the spot and not at midnight or the following noon. I expect it will be in Santa's doctor bag soon enough.

PRAYER TO WINTER

Do not abandon us!
We who fear your fury
love your coverlet of snow.
We who cower at the bus stop
love the ice beneath our skates.
We who daily deplore your omnipotence
weep at your unseasonal melting.

We will push our skis uphill for you,
chain our tires, jump our batteries,
scarf and beard our cheeks,
bury the curves of our bodies
for you.

And we will shovel
until the rhythm of our shoveling
exalts us in your presence.
Until the stroke of our blade
And the smoke of our breath
blows honest and pure, until
the Niagara of our nose is frozen,
our muscles sinewy and warm,
and we burst through the door
with an explosion of stomping
and clapping, throwing open
ourselves, yelling, "I'm
home!" I'm home!"

Do not abandon us,
as we
have abandoned you.

Woodpecker Winter
(January 2015)

I am a bird watcher, venturing into the wild with binoculars in search of the elusive. My wife is a bird-whisperer. She lures wild birds to our kitchen window at the corner of Girard and Lincoln.

Over the years she has constructed an elegant complex of feeders that bring her pleasure. The resulting banquet has enticed an especially colorful company this year since she added a suet feeder, a meal especially nutritious to woodpeckers.

Years ago a pair of downy woodpeckers moved into one of the columns holding up our driveway pergola. They drilled a three-inch hole and moved in. I caulked up the hole with plastic wood. They drilled it right back out. I conceded and they became neighbors, raising their young.

So it made sense that downy woodpeckers were the first to arrive at the suet feeder, but soon another began to appear. At first we were not sure if it was the hairy woodpecker, as the markings are virtually identical to the downy. Then we saw them together on the feeder at the same time, and the size difference was clear, like a sparrow versus a robin. Hairy it was.

Males and females of both species are now regulars, males distinguished by a splash of red paint on the back of the head, so now we have two woodpecker families in the neighborhood. What could be better?

Then the red-bellied woodpecker arrived. I recognized it right away from my birding excursions along the Mississippi River near Frontenac, where we also see the red-headed woodpecker. I never expected to see one in the neighborhood, but here it is. It has very fine black and white horizontal striations on its back. The robin-size male sports a wash of red across the top of the head from beak to nape, and a white belly with a reddish wash at the edges, subtly beautiful.

I assumed it was passing through, but it too has become a regular, loving the suet Susan puts out, visiting shortly after dawn and sometimes during the day, now a male and female, so we have yet another woodpecker family in the 'hood. What could be better?

Then last week a pileated woodpecker arrived. It is the pterodactyl of woodpeckers, at seventeen inches nearly twice as tall as the red-bellied or hairy. "Pileated" means "helmeted," a reasonable description. It landed on the suet feeder, it's size and weight tipping it nearly horizontal. One more neighborhood woodpecker resident! Could anything be better?

Then the massive ivory-billed woodpecker arrived! Another head taller, blacker, tipping the feeder and my brain totally upside down! A bird of the southern forests, long believed extinct! And yet....

Just kidding! But if it were not extinct, I'm sure it would turn up at Susan's woodpecker-magnet. Our winter back yard now resembles our house during Christmas dinner. Colorful adults and children and grandchildren jostle at the table over the feast placed before them. All anticipate the arrival of the red-hatted bearer of joy.

"Nature, Red in Tooth and Claw"
(February 2015)

Alfred Lord Tennyson, England's beloved Poet Laureate during much of Queen Victoria's reign, wrote a line in his poem "In Memoriam" that the world remembers still: "Nature, red in tooth and claw."

That image was much on my mind as I inspected a trail of feathers and blood left near our backyard bird feeder by a raptor visitor, a Cooper's hawk. The remains were of a house sparrow. That's happy news for us, as beloved cardinals and woodpeckers are bigger, ergo more meat for the Cooper's beak and claws. But the House or English sparrow *(passer domesticus)* is the prolific pig at our trough, and we are glad to be rid of one if not more.

We have been noting occasional visits of the Cooper's hawk *(Accipiter cooperii)* at the corner of Girard and Lincoln for the past several winters. It is similar to its slightly smaller cousin the sharp-shinned hawk, but with a larger head, batman cowl and fearsome red eyes, both species designed specially to prey on birds. Short, wide wings and a long narrow tail provide astonishing maneuverability through forest branches in pursuit of flying prey.

A sure sign that the bird hawk has appeared is the sudden absence of backyard birds and birdsong. Sparrow chatter vanishes, along with the sparrows themselves, as do the woodpeckers, cardinals, nuthatches, chickadees, huddling in the safe confines of spruce and euonymus branches. No bird wants to meet a Cooper's hawk for lunch.

Noticing the sudden quiet, if I peer into the back yard and often enough there it is, red-eyed and malevolent, roosting in the cedar hedge or on a branch of the boulevard maple overlooking the feeder, if not springing off the ground after a surprise attack.

If you sense mixed feelings about his arrival, you are correct. We revile house sparrows, English imports that, like we humans, crowd out much of native life, not only at the feeder, but by colonizing native nests. We love our array of native birds that we patiently lure to the feeder only to be shouldered aside by hovering hordes of house sparrows.

So if the Cooper's feasted only on house sparrows we would be thrilled. But his bloody eyes, hooked beak, and needle-sharp claws are indiscriminate, with not enough lunch meetings to control the booming sparrow population.

We are forced, therefore, to bring forth our own "nature, red in tooth and claw" in the form of a sparrow trap, which we planned to put out in the spring. But the instructions have given my wife pause. Once a bunch of birds have entered the trap (baited with millet), we are to don a glove and separate and release any good birds – native sparrows, chickadees, others, easy enough. Then dump the cage full of house sparrows into a mesh laundry bag, spin it wildly around and around, and then…, smash it into the side of a tree? Maybe more than once? Hmmm. We are not sure we hate house sparrows quite that much. In theory, we should have no compunction controlling sparrow overpopulation. In practice, our predatory conviction weakens when it is our own claws that must redden.

Not to mention, what would we do with the lifeless bodies? Bury them in the yard, where our daughter wouldn't even let us bury the ashes of the family dog (now lying in state in the closet)? Leave them lying on the ground as a warning to their sparrow compeers (actually to attract feral cats)? Or, like the king of the old nursery rhyme, bake them into a pie, singing the while…

Sing a song of sixpence,
A pocket full of rye
Four and twenty sparrows,
Baked in a pie.

We humans have sharp incisors for tearing flesh for food. And like English sparrows, our appetites are gargantuan. Nature, "red in tooth and claw," reminds us we are part of, not apart from, bloody natural cycles. So hurrah for the Cooper's hawk who surprises our dormant predatory nature, reminding us that even our high-minded pursuits of compassion are pursued with fuel gathered by our ravenous claws. Tennyson's full quatrain captures the entire tale:

Who trusted God was love indeed
And love Creation's final law
Tho' Nature, red in tooth and claw
With ravine, shriek'd against his creed.

One of the Five Best
Neighborhoods on Planet Earth
(March 2015)

At a dinner party the other night, we met some recent immigrants and tourists. One young couple had freshly moved to the neighborhood after global corporate peregrinations. The tourists ventured all the way from St. Paul.

All of us agreed ours is one of the five best neighborhoods on the planet. We laughed together, eyes shining, almost giddy with our good luck to live (or visit) here.

The dinner party was hosted by our newest neighbors at Girard and Lincoln. "We flunked the suburbs," they allowed. More giddy laughter, although wine may have been involved.

Another new neighbor arrived for dessert. He had lived and worked for years on the East Coast, but found he can do his job from here just as well with infinitely better housing options. Initially skeptical, he now wishes he had moved here years before. OK, wine was involved.

But even in the cold shower of dawn, we remain dazzled by where we are allowed to live. We caress Lake of the Isles yet are spitting distance from downtown. We are two stoplights from I94 and 35W and unimpeded access to the entire North American continent. MSP airport, rated number one in amenities in the nation, is a bare 20 minutes away if one is compelled to travel. But why? Everything one needs is here.

Where are the other four great neighborhoods? I have no idea, though similar neighborhoods must exist with comparable access, amenities, variety and welcoming spirit. Just like, mathematically, there is certain to be more than one planet in the universe as generously habitable as our beloved blue-green Mother Earth. If your telescope locates one, let me know. Meanwhile, I'm staying put.

Sparks of Fire
(April 2015)

"My fingers emit sparks of fire with expectation of my future labors," William Blake wrote in a letter to a friend in 1800. My fingers do as well, anticipating writing, snow shoveling or leaf raking. But I am writing now about literal sparks of fire. They radiated off my fingertips and between my fingers

and off my hands and body and those of my companions the starlit night of March 14, 2015 in the Gulf of Mexico off the coast of southwest Florida.

Florida. A state whose politics would insult Neanderthals. Where the current governor has banned the use of the phrase "climate change" and "global warming" by his state staff, even – especially – those charged with preparing for the impacts of climate change on a state particularly vulnerable.

A state whose race relations make the Twin Cities look like Oz.

A state where Big Sugar and the current governor conspire to overthrow federal law to prevent implementation of an Everglades protection plan funded by, you guessed it, taxpayers in Minnesota and elsewhere, to induce the welfare queen Florida government to do the right thing.

Rick Scott is the Scott Walker of the south, an idiot in governor's clothing. No one should visit his state.

Nevertheless, there I was, standing in the dark Gulf surf, eyes wide with amazement.

For over 30 years my wife's family has gathered at a particular resort for a week in spring to celebrate family togetherness, and in so doing I have found my own delights. Birdwatching at dawn. Cooking breakfast for grandchildren. Swimming in the bright Gulf sunlight. Sleeping after dinner in the humid dark.

So when my wife roused me from bed to say I *must* come out to the Gulf, I was grumpy. No way, I said, falling back asleep. You must, she said, glowing with persistence, there is phosphorescence there, you can see it, like stars in the water!

I had heard of this phenomenon, bioluminescence emitted by microscopic dinoflagellates that light up when disturbed. Ocean sailors tell stories of glowing wakes at night. Our eldest daughter once described a night dive in the Virgin Islands years ago, an illuminated dream she would never forget.

So with my wife's prodding, her eyes lit with fire, I stumbled down the sandy path toward the murmuring shore where other family members gathered in ghostly dark.

I already told you what I found. Wave an arm in the unusually warm Gulf and a blue-white foam followed. Wave the other arm, the same. Dive and a greenish white hood shrouded you. But the most breathtaking act was simplest. Lift a hand slowly through the surface with fingers spread wide and watch sparks of fire roll back into the sea.

According to Wikipedia, dinoflagellates were first described by Henry Baker in 1753 as *"Animalcules which cause the Sparkling Light in Sea Water."* They are sometimes called "fire algae." I call them, mimicking Blake, *illuminations.*

There must be an evolutionary purpose for such behavior. But I think these sparks exist to get humans out of bed to illuminate our lives with astonishment. Like a good poem, a great painting, ethereal music or stunning sculpture, blue green light in warm gulf currents enriches one's sense of an already incomprehensibly rich living world.

There are other natural phenomena to celebrate in Florida, where Ponce de Leon once sought eternal life. Canoodling manatees. Leaping bat-winged rays. Flocks of royal terns with Clark Gable slicked back hairdos. Black-capped skimmers with outsized lower jaws like my grandfather's when smoking his pipe. Tall white ibis strolling on red stick legs probing sand and surf with red decurved beaks.

But better see them fast, before the governor and his developer minions erode what remains of nature's brilliance here. Though even if he succeeds in fully cementing the state coast-to-coast with ignorance, expect these tiny dinoflagellates to prosper in the warmer world the governor ignores. I can see it now: waves of literal enlightenment washing over the state capital in Tallahassee, blue-green sparks of fire radiating off the submerged capitol dome.

The Goodlands in Spring
(April 2014)

It's like discovering flowers growing on the moon. Yet here they are, scattered over cracked gray clay hills like random jewels. The Gumbo Lily, not a true lily but a member of the evening primrose family, has four large heart-shaped petals in dense white blossoms, heartbreakingly lovely snuggled against this impossible, murderous soil, the stuff of cat litter. The western Dakotas are the easternmost limit of this flower's range, and what a lovely symbol for the many surprises a spring trip to Badlands National Park offers visitors.

My friends and I arrived at the Circle View Guest Ranch, a year-round bed-and-breakfast operation near the heart of Badlands National Park, in the flowering of mid-May. Six miles south of the main park entrance at the tiny town of Interior, we were greeted by owners Phil and Amy Kruse, their two young children and the family burro, Duster.

The approach to the ranch is anything but prepossessing, the low-slung modern ranch house disappearing over the far rim. But inside all is warm friendliness, pleasant rooms, great views, delicious breakfasts cooked by Amy while managing to nurse her youngest, and engaging conversations with Phil, son of two generations of hardy ranchers. Those talks sometimes turn to the government's maddening protection of the endangered black-footed ferret and the prairie dogs it preys upon, which has made ranching "impossible" around here. Which is why Phil and his brother and friends hand-built the Circle View on the family's 3,000 acres.

The arrangement allows them to remain living on the

land they love by soaking up the dollars of happy guests like my group of four and others from as close as Iowa and as distant as Boston and Arizona. After three breakfasts together, and post-dinner bouts of foosball and ping pong in the game room, we were all firm friends.

Outside, the eroded moonscape of our arrival gives way past lily-dotted clay humps to the surprise of the White River Valley below, named for its white clay sediment, coming alive with greening pastures and budding cottonwoods and willow, evening serenades of coyotes and a dawn chorus of lark sparrows, a rooster, bellowing cows and wild turkeys gobbling for mates, a working bottomlands farm.

Our guide is David Astin, my Minneapolis birding guru, retired wildlife science teacher and skilled nature photographer who recently spent nearly two months living in and photographing the park. He knows every nook of the park's spectacular wedding cake geology and where to find abundance in a place most would see as wasteland but what architect Frank Lloyd Wright called, in 1935, "a revelation." For the next two days we drove and hiked the park's varied landscapes, discovering proof of Wright's assertion over and over, beginning with geology and ending with astronomy.

Up to now I had never wondered about the odd name of Wall, S.D., the town famous for its drugstore a short drive north of the park. Now I know. It is located on the treeless plain just above the dramatically eroded "wall" of the ancient White River watershed, a steep descent of gullies, pyramids, organ pipes and other unusual formations that are the famous Badlands scenery, still eroding an inch a year.

The generic geological term "badlands" originated from the name given this region by early French trappers. The White River Badlands, approximately 100 miles long and 3 to 5 miles wide, form the core of Badlands National Park sandwiched between Buffalo Gap National Grasslands and the Pine Ridge Ogalala Lakota Nation, which has a joint management agreement for the southern section of the park.

A specific geological oddity found here are "sod tables," mesas with tops as small as a dining room table or as large as a cornfield, covered with blowing prairie grasses because the sod resists the erosion below. In the old days, farmers would haul a disassembled mower up Hay Butte and reassemble it to cut hay – until the hay blew away in a rough Badlands wind.

Since the end of the "sod busting" era, the Badlands and surrounding mixed grass prairies have become a haven for reintroduced wildlife species. Bison and bighorn sheep flourish, impossible to miss; the black-footed ferret impossible to see but subject of the most talk among the locals. Reintroduced to the park from a remnant population captive-bred in Wyoming, the ferret's survival requires prairie dogs as the primary food source, therefore prairie dogs are also locally protected. That's bad news for ranchers, as prairie dog towns make nasty hoof traps for grazing cattle, but good news for tourists with binoculars.

We viewed with delight several large prairie dog towns where furry families emerged from burrows with blinking babies into the spring morning. And, thanks to Dave's sharp eyes, we saw the tops of the heads of burrowing owls staring back at us with oval yellow eyes from their pirated burrows. We visited all of these on our first morning trip through the park, accompanied by a flock of lark buntings cavorting along the road.

Then back to the Circle View for lunch from our cooler in the arbor.

That afternoon we set out past another prairie dog town thriving inside the human ghost town of Conata to visit the spectacular Sage Creek Wilderness Area, overlooking views of distant eroded bluffs like medieval cities. We continued into the 66,000-acre buffalo grasslands, where herds of bison grazed against bluffs striped pink and yellow and gray. On the way home on Sage Creek Rim Road, a giant bull sauntered by, his winter fur shedding in ragged clumps.

After a robust breakfast the next morning, we departed for a quiet day of meditation on Sheep Mountain Table, rising in the South Unit of the park 36 miles west.

We took our time along the way, pausing to marvel at a red-tailed hawk clasping a 3-foot snake in its talons, and a magnificent ferruginous hawk, the largest in North America, its dark feathered legs forming a V against its white breast.

At roadside sloughs green with spring runoff (dry in summer), we found pairs of long-billed curlews and the striking black and white American avocet busily sweeping its needle-like upturned beak over the mud shallows.

The road up Sheep Mountain Table is not for the faint of car springs, the deeply rutted track requires all-wheel drive. Along the slow, spring-busting way, we drank in the waving prairie grassland and singing meadowlarks. We parked in a scrub oak thicket and set off individually for an hour of private mediation along the rim with hawks soaring below. In the Lakota tradition, we tied colorful strips of cloth onto branches to let the clear winds carry our thoughts and prayers with the passing mountain bluebirds.

On our way back to an early dinner at the Red Rock Cafe in Wall (and an obligatory peek into the carnival known as Wall Drug), we toured the back roads of the Sage Creek Wilderness Area, sighting flocks of white pelicans and pied-billed grebes in the spring ponds and sloughs, 20 antelope passing at full run, and a magnificent golden eagle hunting overhead.

Returning to the rim road with towering clouds building over the Black Hills to the west, we were dazzled by late sun streaming golden light over bison grazing so near to us that we could see symbiotic cowbirds hunting for insects among their fur. Then a lone antelope dove under a nearby fence at full speed: "That's what they do out here," said Dave, "which is why their backs look like they've had a haircut!"

On the Badlands Loop Road back toward "home" at the Circle View, Dave had one more treat for us. He pulled into the final overlook parking lot before the road plunged down the "wall." With the sky now in full darkness, he invited us out of the van, then said, "Now look up."

I have seen stars before, and the Milky Way flowing overhead, but nothing – ever – like this. In what is said to be the continent's clearest air, the stars were indeed a "revelation," a blanket of white-hot starlight containing roving bands of satellites and shooting stars, one of which broke in two before us in full Fourth of July fireworks celebration.

Indeed, mid-May in the Badlands felt like a national holiday, a time when we could celebrate a place still distant from the pollution and lightscape of encroaching civilization. A place not at all the Badlands described by early explorers, but, instead, as many Lakota call it, *Mako Washte*, The Goodlands.

(Reprinted from the *StarTribune*)

A Tar Sands March from the Neighborhood
(June 2015)

On Saturday, June 6, my wife and I marched with four thousand other souls from the banks of the Mississippi River to the State Capitol, the first shrouded in morning mist, the second shrouded with construction scaffolding. We were rallying to say "no" to expanding the matrix of pipelines across Minnesota's northern border bringing foul tar sands oil to southern refineries.

I drove to St. Paul in my fossil-fueled powered car to don my apron of MN350.org and gather petition signatures. My wife and friend Marian Moore did better, bicycling to the Green Line, although the Green line is also somewhat powered by fossil fuels.

So are we hypocrites? Wasting energy? Our time? Or both? You decide.

Start by googling photos of the Alberta tar sands. Read, for random example, this article in *Business Insider,* "These Pictures May Give you Nightmares about The Canada Oil Sands." It includes this sentence: "We're not saying the project is good or bad. We're just saying the scale and severity of what's happening in Alberta will make your spine tingle."

Or read this selection from Wikipedia: *"The Athabasca River is the largest freshwater delta in the world but with Suncor and Syncrude leaking tail ponds the amount of polluted water will exceed 1 billion cubic meters by 2020."*

It gets worse. Tar sands oil is 17 percent more carbon intensive than normal oil. As I write this, "In a rare, large consensus, more than 100 scientists unite to say expanding tar sands will be catastrophic for the climate and environment." We marchers in St. Paul are saying – *tar sands oil is bad for us all!*

If any of you have children, be active, be very, very active. Imagine the hottest, most hideous humid day of a Minnesota summer, so hot you perspire freely sitting still. Now imagine two months of such days, then three, then four. As Dr. James Hansen has said, "the Southern half of the United State will be uninhabitable," while Minnesota becomes the climate of... Missouri? And after that...? Never mind the plants and wildlife that can't adapt, how are you going to live on Lowry Hill?

HLP readers understand this crisis, and I am happy to report so do our local elected leaders, all active the climate fight, as are many local businesses. For example, Golden Valley-based Mortenson Construction is the largest installer of solar and wind power in the United States, the fastest growing sector of the country's energy market.

Will we stop uncontrollable climate catastrophe in time? Yes, if three things happen simultaneously, all of which require your participation and support.

Many speakers were Native Americans who live with the direct impacts of these rapacious developments and are leading the charge against them. One was Winona LaDuke, founder of Honor the Earth and the Indigenous Environmental Network, who has worked for decades to call attention to better ways to manage our planet than tearing out its heart.

We also heard from Bill McKibben, the Martin Luther King of climate change. A *New Yorker* journalist, he founded 350.org, now a global grass roots climate advocacy organization, when he realized writing articles and books was not enough.

A surprise powerhouse speaker was Alilah Sanders-Reed, a student at Macalester College. She roused us all with a plea from and for her generation facing the brunt of the climate calamity.

We live in the midst of a great war. The old, extractive industries that built modern civilization are fighting the green energy future that can sustain us. Can we adapt in time? The battle is joined. The answer is up to us.

Up at the Lake and Managing It
(July 2015)

I write this on an island at the intersection of three Great Lakes, Superior, Huron and Michigan. Mackinac is pronounced today "mack-in-naw," the legacy of French voyageurs who didn't have an "ack" sound for the Anishinabek word Michilimackinac, which means Great Turtle, snapping turtle in real life. So I am standing on Turtle Island as described in the Anishinabek creation story, as do we all. The view overlooking Lake Huron is as beautiful as any I know. But the view under the surface of the lake tells a different story, one we all need to hear.

Before arriving here I stopped to visit my sister at the old family cottage on the south shore of Green Bay. When I arrived I encountered a gaggle of young boys who had been fishing, as I did as a boy for perch and bass. They showed me with disgust their stringer of Round Gobies, a recent invasive fish that eagerly takes bait, making it difficult now to catch desirable game fish.

Meanwhile, in the upper reaches of Lakes Michigan and Huron the delicious native whitefish grow smaller and smaller. A fish that has sustained communities in the region for millenniums is losing the war with invasive zebra mussels, those half-inch razor blades from the Caspian Sea that arrived secreted in the ballast water of visiting ocean freighters, the same route taken by round gobies in more recent years. Zebra mussels, and now their cousin Quagga mussels, filter out lake nutrients at the base of the food chain. Round Gobies actually eat zebra mussels, but sadly not enough to dent the population.

On the plus side, Coho and Chinook salmon thrive in the lakes' deep, cold waters. The salmon are neither native nor invasive, but planted by the Michigan Department of Natural Resources in a desperate attempt to control another invasive, the alewife. Alewives are a small Atlantic herring that swam up the Welland Canal that breached the natural barrier of Niagara Falls between the Atlantic and Great Lakes ecosystems. They discovered an awesome new home with plenty of food and few predators. By the 1960's alewives had so prospered that once I saw a 30 mile-long raft of dead alewives visible from the air. Periodically overwhelmed by ecosystem limits, they died in droves and washed up in reeking dunes on Chicago, Milwaukee and Michigan beaches. Desperate for a solution, state of Michigan scientists introduced Coho and Chinook, who it turned out *loved* to dine on alewives! So ecological balance was restored, creating on the side a billion-dollar sport fishing industry in Lake Michigan and Huron. Now if we can only keep invasive Asian Carp out of the Great Lakes, today's freshwater ecosystem battle, the outcome far from certain.

All of which reminds me of the sea lamprey, the terror of my childhood growing up swimming in Green Bay. Its ancestors also discovered the Welland Canal. Called the "vampire of the Great Lakes," the lamprey consists a circular buzz saw mouth attached to an empty sock of a body a foot long. It grinds its teeth into the side of a fish (or human) and sucks the blood, a super-efficient killing machine that has decimated defenseless native Lake trout populations among others. When I was a boy we buried dead fish up and down the shore daily that bore the telltale white circles of lamprey predation. Once a lamprey fastened to my sister's leg, another time to a neighbor's, who exited the bay screaming.

In the 1950's desperate wizards at the Wisconsin DNR developed a species-specific poison administered into the headwaters of streams where the eels spawn. The lamprey population plummeted and has been under control ever since. Until now, as the lamprey has developed a breeding population in the fast-flowing St. Mary's River connecting lakes Superior and Huron. So the war continues, now with helicopters and GPS.

What should we humans learn from these invasions and defenses of our beloved Great Lakes? First, "Nature" no longer exists. We no longer have ecosystems, only *managed ecosystems*. We broke 'em, we gotta fix 'em. Bison in Yellowstone, wolves in northern states, too many white-tailed deer, destructive exotic earthworms the north woods, forests attacked by invasive Dutch elm beetles and emerald ash borers and beech blight, lakes infected with milfoil, zebra mussels, round gobies, alewives, sea lampreys and more.

And now the earth's atmosphere, invaded by fossil carbon, mercury and sulfates from the burning of once buried coal, oil and natural gas.

The Abrahamic creation story says that on the sixth day, as reported in the King James version of Genesis: *And God said, Let us make man in our image, after our likeness: and let them have dominion over the fish of the sea, and over the fowl of the air, and over the cattle, and over all the earth, and over every creeping thing that creepeth upon the earth.*

The authors of Genesis got it right. No longer is there a creature who creepeth over the earth whose fate is not in the palm of our collective human hands. Yours and mine. We do have dominion. The question is how we will use it. We have learned to manage the Great Lakes. Will we learn to manage the earth's atmosphere? We can do it, but only if we believe.

❧

Powwow Summer

(August 2015)

There are powwows and there are powwows. Some are glitzy contest affairs, with dancers from around North America competing for serious prize money. Others are "traditional," a homecoming for the local band, friends and welcome visitors.

My favorite traditional pow wow is "Honor the Earth," a homecoming for the Lac Courte Oreilles nation in the pristine forest near Hayward, Wisconsin, always the third weekend of July. The powwow ground behind the new tribal college is a lovely circular arbor surrounded by embracing white and red pines, where bald eagles soar overhead.

This year two of my former students were to be honored, so I had an extra incentive to make the drive to the tea-colored rivers and lakes around Hayward. Thelma Nayquonabe was to be honored on Saturday for her persistent work rebuilding the Anishinabe (Ojibwe) language. A pioneer teacher and organizer, she is now mother bear for her people. I arrived just in time for the noon honoring ceremony, and was surprised and pleased to be invited into the center of the circle with Thelma's friends where tribal officials wrapped Thelma in a beautiful quilt. I was surprised again to find there my Minneapolis friend Larry Long. Turns out Larry, a troubadour in the tradition of Woody Guthrie and Pete Seeger, had been working with Thelma to connect tribal elders and children through song, part of a Smithsonian recording series.

After the ceremony, all the audience was invited to dance in Thelma's honoring song. I found my feet rising and falling to the drum, though I had wrecked an ankle in a bicycle crash only a few days prior. When the second song picked up speed, I did too.

On a break from dancing I consumed an Indian taco – taco trimmings piled on thick, delicious frybread – then drove a few miles up the road in to visit other friends in Cable, home of the Birkebeiner cross-country ski race in winter and the Chequamegon fat tire bicycle race in summer. The tiny town teemed with bicyclists consuming wood-fired pizza and locally-brewed beer at an outdoor beer garden. I skipped the beer to swim in a silken nearby lake, where I had the opportunity to rescue an elderly couple whose motor had died.

The following day I attended the honoring ceremony for another former student, Thelma's sister Trixie Nayquon-abe, who tragically passed away a few years prior. The give-away was organized by her daughter Kelly, now a mother and grandmother whom I remembered as a skilled jingle dress dancer. Kelly was the one who had called to invite me this year.

During a scheduled break in the drumming, Kelly spread a large quilt on the grass in the powwow circle and covered it with a stack of folded quilts, woven baskets, maple syrup, and bags of hand-harvested wild rice. Then the powwow MC read off a list of people to receive these gifts in Trixie's honor. When I heard my name, I was again surprised and honored. I received a beautiful, colorful quilt stenciled with Trixie's name, which I wear around my shoulders as I write this.

Leaving for home that afternoon, I stopped at one of the many craft booths to purchase an intricate dreamcatcher and a tiny pair of hand-beaded moccasins for my newest grandson, due to be born in August. The first will ensure him good dreams, the second will warm his feet for his first dances on Mother Earth.

Honor the Earth powwow is open to families, friends, dancers and visitors of all skills and colors – white clouds, red dust, brown fur, green skirts, black arms, blue sky. All are welcome to feel the drum vibrate in the chest, "the heartbeat of the earth." Next July, or the next or the next, visit the LCO nation and re-learn how to honor the earth with your steps.

End of Summer, Preparing for a Fall?
(September 2015)

These September days sink spirits. Sunrise and sunset rage crimson thru scrims of smoke and ash from colossal Western wildfires. The full moon drips blood.

Are these signs of Armageddon said to befalleth the earth? Yes they are. But I am happy to report, not yet in Minnesota, not in our neighborhood.

We have long heard about "The Big One," the massive earthquake due any day now on the San Andreas fault on California's west coast, not far from where our son now lives with his young family. But did you read the article in *The New Yorker*, July 20, 2017 issue, about "The REALLY Big One?" A 9.5 earthquake and tsunami of epic size and destructiveness is statistically overdue to flatten the Pacific Northwest, collapsing Portland and Seattle! It will make the havoc of Fukashima seem child's play.

Bad news for our adult children who live in Seattle, one with four children plus a husband we like and children we love. I sent them a copy of the article, with a Grumpy Grandpa note advising them, no panic, just sell the house *immediately* and move to Minnesota! They can live in our basement with pets and kids until they find other accommodations. Or I'll move into the basement!

An over-the-top freak-out? Read the article.

Back to *The New Yorker*, this time the Aug 24, 2017 issue,

the deeply researched article by Elizabeth Kolbert on the upcoming global climate negotiations in Paris this December, "global collapse" hanging in the balance.

Is she exaggerating? Read the article.

Do I sound like a scold? Well, I'm old and scared. So if those two words combine to make "scold," so be it, I'm a scold.

What does all this have to do with the neighborhood? Nothing! That's the good news! Even a glance around our hotter, drought–plagued, glacier-melting planet reveals that Minnesota is *the safest place for humans to live on Planet Earth!* Touched by the Great Lakes and fourteen thousand smaller ones, Minnesota is rich in farmland to the southern horizon and abundant, if changing, forests to the north, with plentiful sunlight and wind to power our region without fossil fuels. The state's smart, hard-working, four season-loving citizens practice innovative business and progressive government, where the challenges of the future are not ignored but embraced.

I hope you are as ecstatic as I am to live in part of world better prepared, and more resistant to disaster, that any other.

My Missouri friend Jim Bogan begs to disagree on this last point. A resident of the heart of the ancient Ozark Mountains, he gleefully argues that the next "Big One" will be an earthquake issuing from Missouri's ancient New Madrid fault. It is going to get us. The previous one, in 1811, was the largest earthquake east of the Rockies. Actually four quakes trembling over two weeks, among other wreckage it ran the Mississippi River backwards.

But I have looked into this worrisome matter and assure readers its future shock will not do damage here. From Wiki:

In a report filed in November 2008, the U.S. Federal Emergency Management Agency warned that a serious earth–

quake in the New Madrid Seismic Zone could result in "the highest economic losses due to a natural disaster in the United States," further predicting "widespread and catastrophic" damage across Alabama, Arkansas, Illinois, Indiana, Kentucky, Mississippi, Missouri, and particularly Tennessee, where a 7.7 magnitude quake or greater would cause damage to tens of thousands of structures affecting water distribution, transportation systems, and other vital infrastructure.

Minnesota is not mentioned! So add "earthquake-free zone" to the state's long list of benefits. Relative to the rest of the planet, our city and region are simply not disaster prone. The occasional tornado or blizzard? Child's play. Winter? The snowplows are sharp and ready to roll.

But the state does need to prepare for a flood of refugees from climate change, tsunamis and earthquake occurring elsewhere. Will there be room at the inn? We'll make room. Better crowded into a basement with Minnesota's bracing four seasons than in any of the hot and hellish alternatives.

Merry El Niño

(November 2015)

As I write this, the neighborhood continues a lovely fall run of 10-20 degrees Fahrenheit above normal. Although some snow may arrive by winter solstice and Christmas, extremely warm temperatures are forecast to continue through much of meteorological winter.

The reason is "El Niño", the warm phase of the El Niño Southern Oscillation {ENSO} in the Pacific Ocean. But that is only the recent scientific explanation. Older views may well have more currency today. Here's the story of one.

In 1978 I traveled to Peru in search of stories, including a visit to the newly excavated palace at Chan Chan, capital of the Chimu empire. Chan Chan ("sun sun") is a massive urban and palace complex that thrived from about 900CE to 1470CE (more than twice as long as the United States) until defeated by the Inca empire invading from the Andes, then by the Spanish invading from Europe, who moved the city somewhat inland to what is now modern-day Trujillo.

The abandoned city covers nearly 20 square miles on the Pacific coast, the palace alone more than two square miles, all built from adobe walls that look today like endless ribbons of melted ice cream. What caused the adobe to erode in a city situated in the rain shadow of the Andes, one of the driest places on earth?

When I asked locals that question in 1978, the immediate answer was "El Niño," a weather event I had never heard of before. Every fifty years or so, they said, the skies mysteriously opened into a massive, unaccountable cloudburst of rain, never before seen by the generations living there. After the palace and city were abandoned, no one was left to repair the walls so they slowly melted under the rare rainfalls. Today a few archaeologists are finally studying and salvaging Chan Chan and its story.

The origin of the term El Niño, then, has to do with when those rare storms occurred, generally around Christmastime; hence "El Nino" with a capital N, the coming of "the Christ Child."

Today when we hear meteorologists chatter on about El Niño, we think about increasingly frequent superheated Pacific waters, the worst events now accompanied by epic rain eventts and bleached coral and befuddled sea life (The intense El Niño event of 1998 caused an estimated

16% of the world's coral reef systems to die).

But another explanation should also color our current understanding of what this year's massive El Nino portends, forecast to be bigger and hotter and more destructive than the one in 1998. Could it be the "rough beast, its hour come round at last," that William Butler Yeats prophesied in "The Second Coming"?

Do you remember that poem from high school English class? Published in 1921, it emerged from the aftermath of the epic slaughter of the first World War to somehow anticipate the genocidal madness of the second, the post War environmental and climate crises, even the xenophobia of recent Republican Presidential debates. Listen to the prophesy:

THE SECOND COMING

Turning and turning in the widening gyre
The falcon cannot hear the falconer;
Things fall apart; the center cannot hold;
Mere anarchy is loosed upon the world,
The blood-dimmed tide is loosed, and everywhere
The ceremony of innocence is drowned;
The best lack all conviction, while the worst
Are full of passionate intensity.
Surely some revelation is at hand;
Surely the Second Coming is at hand.
The Second Coming! Hardly are these words out
When a vast image out of Spiritus Mundi
Troubles my sight: somewhere in the sands of the desert
A shape with lion body and the head of a man,
A gaze blank and pitiless as the sun,
Is moving its slow thighs, while all about it
Reel shadows of the indignant desert birds.
The darkness drops again; but now I know

That twenty centuries of stony sleep
Were vexed to nightmare by a rocking cradle,
And what rough beast, its hour come round at last,
Slouches toward Bethlehem to be born?'

As the most hopeful of holiday seasons swirls ahead of us like the snow we long for, let us embrace the vision of El Niño sleeping in that rocking cradle – love for one's neighbor, justice and peace for all, intolerance for the intolerant, and a firm belief that we will protect in time the glories of God's Creation. Amen.

Santa's On His Way!
(December 2015)

The cab arrived right on time at 7:15am. Mr. and Mrs. Coyote were packed and ready. This would be our first Christmas in 48 years of parenthood not at home for Santa's arrival. We were flying to rainy Seattle to spend Christmas day with our two children and four grandchildren resident there. We were curious to learn if Santa's famously stout frame could navigate rickety wood-stove chimneys in Seattle as he does so expertly in the north country built right for sleighs and reindeer.

We were ready in spite of a sleepless Christmas Eve. At three in the morning we both heard a noise. In the bedroom. Maybe in the wall. Maybe under the bed. A plaster rattling noise.

Such a sound is unnervingly familiar to any who have spent nights in drafty summer cabins, cheap motel rooms, or an ancient Volkswagen camper with a raccoon gnawing on the drain. A mouse? A rat? A chipmunk? Squirrel? Raccoon again?

As I swept my iPhone flashlight under the bed, revealing only a dusty pile of forgotten wrapping paper, my wife bolted upright with a blast of illumination. "It's reindeer!" she exclaimed.

Of course! How could we have forgotten so soon? What other animal makes mysterious house noises on Christmas Eve?

With that comforting thought, we flipped off the lights and fell back to sleep, visions of sugar plums baiting rodent traps dancing in our heads.

How our imaginations have atrophied since the last of our children abandoned the house for adulthood, and now lure us to distant, mysterious lands. Really, why would *anyone* live in rainy Seattle or drought-plagued California? OK, I get New Mexico (the sunsets! the chiles!). Still, here we are, running to catch a Settle-bound plane on Christmas day.

In the airport lounge, we sat with other bleary-eyed grandparents clutching bulging bags of gifts. Our bags bulged with gifts too, for grandchildren ages twenty to seven. Books of course, from Birchbark Books, a vintage book from Magers and Quinn for our son-in-law, iPhone cases from the Uptown Apple store for the plugged-in grands and to repay the geniuses at the Genius bar who spent an hour and a half on Christmas eve cleaning out junk from my beloved MacBook Air so I could write this.

As we boarded the plane and settled into our seats, we felt exhausted but pleased that at least one reindeer remembered to make his presence known by gnawing on the plaster, or the wiring, or both. We deserved the disturbance, as we had failed to put out cookies, carrots and eggnog to slake reindeer hunger and thirst, a traditional snack we had offered faithfully for 48 years. They had a right to be ornery.

As we flew, we peered out the window to watch Santa and his reindeer gallop westward with us over the mountains and through the rainclouds to grandchildren's house we go. One reindeer shot us a sharp raised eyebrow as he pulled. We gestured back our apologies. We will not forget you again!

For Love of Ice
(February 2016)

On February 6th our daughter called from Seattle (actually she texted): The city had a snowstorm and is completely shut down. No one even biked to work, streets too icy. Schools closed, so the kids played happily in the snow all day. A rare winter delight in rainy Seattle.

Her call reminded me to look out our kitchen window into the back yard. When that daughter's family visited over the Christmas holidays, her eight-year-old twins spent most of their days playing in our routine miracle of snow. Several reminders of that feverish activity linger in the form of a crumbling snow fort and the sturdy body of Mr. Snowman absent now his head and torso.

Delight in winter ice blossomed further as Susan and I strolled Lake of the Isles the evening of the Luminary Loppet. We arrived after dark, lake ice shining like polished slate under streetlights and partial moonlight. The organizers of the event had roughed up an ice trail so pedestrians could venture forth on the magical lake highway with reasonable stability, as the rest of the lake, swept clean of snow cover by wind, was slippery as eel skin. We marveled once again at the glowing luminaria spaced apart with mathematical precision, plus towers of ice elegant as classical Greek columns, an ice sculpture garden, the opaque upright slabs of Icehenge and an Egyptian pyramid of ice, all illuminated with internal candlelight, a splendor of ice and light possible only in the north country.

Fortunately for Luminary planners and visitors, lake ice was thick and firm in spite of unseasonable rain and many abnormal above-freezing days. More than enough sub-freezing nights made the ice strong enough to bear the weight of 10,000 visitors without complaint, plus freeze the many marvels of Icecropolis.

Ice makes it all possible. But how?

Did you know that ice is considered a mineral? And, unusual in the mineral kingdom, ice, the solid phase of water, is substantially less dense than its liquid phase, its hexagonal crystalline structure astonishingly strong and light. Meaning ice floats, not sinks. And because ice floats, it insulates any life below the frozen surface instead of freezing to the bottom and killing it. This magical property, "floating solid water," is a fundamental reason we exist on planet earth today.

The nature of ice was on my mind as we returned the following afternoon to stroll the lake in sunlight. Only a few visitors walked with us, along with the beaver-like activity of Luminary volunteers disassembling their evening marvels. The lake was sunstruck, windless and quiet. We delighted in scooting the hollow remains of luminaria over the shiny black surface like curling stones, listening as the musical bass notes receded into the distance. We augmented that sound with trebles by propelling smaller shards along the frozen surface, an ice orchestra.

Susan lay down and stretched out on the smooth black ice to inspect the depths below, but it proved too thick to allow her to see fishy life swimming below. But on our walk back toward home we noticed several natural ice windows that themselves resembled wondrous fish.

Scientific quandaries about ice remain. Why, for example, in outer space is hexagonal crystalline ice, the predominant form found on Earth, so rare? While scientists search for answers at the outer limits of our universe, our neighborhood lakes freely offer up earthly ice amazements. Because liquid water, when frozen, takes on the properties of a floating solid, we humans can stroll and skate and ski and twirl upon it. Enterprising neighbors can build Icehenge illuminated by candlelight. And, if one is patient, one can hear an orchestra, or catch a fish.

🥢

Deep Travel: The Pilgrimage Within
(March 2016)

My latest book is a memoir describing my forty-year love affair with the voice of a poet who lived in a cave in the Tiantai Mountains of China 1200 years ago. His poems have been so compelling to me that, in 2006, I traveled to China to seek the cave where he was said to have lived and from where his poems echoed so unexpectedly in my life. After many adventures, we arrived at the cave, and I discovered why that poet's voice meant so much to me. That trip became the core of *Seeking the Cave: A Pilgrimage to Cold Mountain*, published in 2014 by Milkweed Editions in a handsome hardbound edition.

Last month the book was published in paperback, and I'm back on the road telling its story. But since that first publication, and well after the seven years it took to write and edit the book, I still remain puzzled by a question that pilgrimage raised for me, what I have come to call "Deep Travel." Bear with me.

We travel for many reasons: curiosity, adventure, challenge, education, excitement, relaxation, of course necessity. We attend reunions with family and friends. We seek warmer suns or better snows or deeper roots or better jobs. But once or twice in a lifetime, if one is lucky, one may find oneself called to travel not from without but from within. Such a trip is not simply an adventure or migration, but a pilgrimage.

In our thinly secular society, pilgrimage seems a medieval or ultra-religious practice. We think of Chaucer's *Canterbury Tales,* or the crowded once-in-a-lifetime return to Mecca of contemporary Muslims, or the handful of Catholic friends who hike the Camino de Santiago de Compostela in Spain. Some Jews and Christians and Muslims feel compelled to visit Jerusalem, other Christians to follow the Pauline trail to ancient Ephesus singing praises to their faith. Some Buddhist and Hindu sects practice pilgrimage to nearby shrines or to the Bodhi tree where Gautama Buddha discovered that suffering is the central fact of the human condition.

Such treks fulfill a religious injunction or vocation or practice. But what if the call to pilgrimage comes from you know not where? What if the call is to discover, not proclaim? Not to answer questions, but to address unanswerable ones?

Such a call came to me twice in my life. In the early 70's I camped with my young family across much of the Great Plains and American Southwest seeking the stories and history of Native America, visiting communities, historic sites and shrines. I realize now I was attempting to fill a palpable void in my education and understanding. I grew up in northeastern Wisconsin near three native reservations, the Oneida, Menominee, and Brotherton, yet knew essentially nothing about them. Meanwhile the drums and protests of the American Indian Movement and marches against the termination of the Menominee reservation had begun to echo in my heart. I felt compelled to fill an emptiness in my head and the heart of the country.

My trip to China felt similar. Han-shan, the mysterious Buddhist hermit poet, is said to have painted his poems on rocks and walls and carved them on bamboo, poems with common-sense humor and self-awareness. Only after he disappeared into a crack in the mountain did others gather his poems into a book. That practice of poetic impermanence felt compelling to me, a joy and grief expressed in art careless of posterity.

I was struck, too, by the medium Han-shan chose to express his sentiments – poetry – a practice at the extremes of language that has enraptured me for much of my life. But why?

On April 11 at Magers and Quinn Booksellers I will tell once more my tale of seeking a cave to find what I did not know I was missing. And I will seek your stories too. What mysterious call might propel you down a trail of self-discovery? Where might such a pilgrimage take you? What emptiness might be filled when you arrive?

Minnesota Safari
(April 2016)

My birding pals David Astin and Frank Wilebski kept telling me that I had to visit the wildlife paradise Frank's brother Larry was creating back home in Lancaster. Where's that? Kittson County. Where's that? Clearly I needed geographic enlightenment.

So in April, Frank arranged for us to spend a weekend at Larry's cabin to prove that all the wildlife stories I was hearing were true. "I guarantee we'll see short-eared owls," David said.

What did we see? Seventy-eight species of birds in one

weekend, including black-billed magpies and gray jays, unusual in Minnesota. Three elk herds. A mother bear and her cubs. The rare local *homo sapiens*, who average but two per square mile throughout the county. But what people! Remnant tribes of hardy Norwegians, Swedes, Germans, Irish, Polish, English, Ukrainian. I felt like we were on safari. I have never seen such varied life in such a brief period of time in a setting that wasn't on an African plain or at the Minnesota Zoo.

Kittson County scratches North Dakota on the west and the Canadian border on the north, as far as a body can go and still speak Minnesotan.

Its flat western upland prairie rubs softly against eastern aspen parkland as glacial Lake Agassiz imperceptibly slopes west toward the Red River. After crossing the county line, we passed through Karlstad, population 794, whose church sign robustly proclaimed, "The Bible said it. I believe it. That's final!"

Larry's place is a few miles outside of Lancaster, population 363, near the geographic center of the county and not far from the collection of Polish immigrant farms where he grew up.

Down a gravel road we passed a mailbox fronting a vanished farmhouse, now housing a roadside badger burrow, before turning onto a two-track to enter "Wilebski's Evergreen Acres," a life's work in progress. Beyond a resting tractor and sleeping snowmobile, the two-story cabin floated on a concrete slab, spartan but warm, with two bedrooms plus a loft for sleeping, a refrigerator for food and beer, and windows, lots of windows, from which to observe the wild world parade by.

A pothole pond abuts one side of the cabin. The other sides are fields and forests studded with 150 bird houses, numerous other critter feeders, trails through the woods and a stream babbling through fields waiting to burst into flower.

Settling in, David aimed his camera through sliding glass

doors toward nearby feeders, "passive birding at its best," he grinned. But our first visitors were not birds but Big Time Human Birders up from the Twin Cities who had stayed here the previous night. With them was Larry Wilebski.

While Dave and one of the visitors traded birding tales, I thumbed a book of wildlife photographs Larry had taken here, including one of a bobcat. For Larry, a father of five who builds buses during the day in nearby Pembina, N.D., this land is "his retirement." He buys 80-acre parcels whenever he can, digs ponds, restores wetlands, plants trees and wildflowers. He's happy to share it with anyone who wants to visit.

After the others left for home, Dave drove us into the flat countryside in afternoon light. At another of Larry's ponds, we observed shoveler ducks, pied-bill grebes and a northern harrier loitering on a sand knoll apparently entranced by the song of an eastern meadowlark. Stopping by another pond, we caught great views of greater yellowlegs, lesser yellow-legs, a pair of wood ducks, ring-necked ducks, mallards, and a hooded merganser among others.

In Lancaster, we made a lazy U-turn on the main street and glided to a stop in front of Dean's Family Diner, one of two restaurants in town, for an early dinner – and glances from the regulars wondering who these strangers could be.

After dinner we drove gravel roads with the sunlight behind us. A pair of marbled godwits stood on their long blue legs in the middle of the road. The ditches rattled with the songs of American chorus frogs, like a comb being stroked with a thumb.

As the light began to fade, we made a final stop along a roadside hay field to observe male sharp-tailed grouse gathered in a lek – a display ground where males strut their stuff in hopes of attracting passing females, like a singles bar on Saturday night. A clump of 14 males vied for center stage, sharp tails up, wings cupped down, bodies parallel to the earth, feet stomping like pistons, shaking their booties. Unfortunately for them, only we birders were mesmerized.

Dawn at Wilebski Acres began like this. At first light, a ruffed grouse drummed his wings against his chest at increasing speed, his mating call, on a log not five feet from the cabin. At 6:30 a.m., the much-anticipated black-billed magpie arrived near the feeder, followed by three gray jays.

Later we watched the courtship flight of a male northern harrier bobbing above and below the tree line, demonstrating for a female his strength and grace. A male wilson's snipe performed an even more dramatic mating flight, as if he were strung on a yo-yo.

In golden morning light we watched a pair of sandhill cranes perform their courtship dance. She suddenly broke forward, dipped her beak into a bunch of grass, threw it wildly up over her head, leaped up off the ground, and turned toward him. They both leaped, crouched, leaped again, heads together facing the sky, joyfully calling. She looked like "a flamenco dancer throwing a rose," Dave said. Up ahead, a coyote dashed across the road and bounded through a neighboring field, pointed ears bouncing above the grass.

As we finished breakfast at Dean's, three farmers wearing overalls and feed caps regaled us with their own back-yard wildlife stories, of cougars sleeping on railroad tracks, a bear playing with a deer spine, elk grazing spring wheat, "a herd can do a lot of damage."

Then we were back on the road. A Wilson's snipe stood on one pale leg on a fence post and, as he turned his head, surprised us with his out-sized bill.

Then we encountered our biggest surprise, a mother bear and two cubs grazing in a roadside field. She glistened silken black, 300 to 500 pounds. When she caught our scent, she reared up on her hind legs and put her front paws together as if in prayer, sniffing. When she sensed we were far enough away to keep us all comfortable, she dropped and shuffled off with her cubs into the brake.

Returning to the cabin, we found a wild turkey wandering the yard and two river otters swimming upstream in the creek. I logged a blissful midday nap in the sun next to the pond, serenaded by choral frog comb strokes, bull frog bass drums and a yellow-bellied sapsucker hammering the power pole's insulator glass – a mating symphony at full volume.

Back on the road later, we encountered an elk herd feeding in thick grass, one of three herds that now roam the county. A massive bull watched over his harem of 14 cows, all with buff-colored butts and oddly inconsequential tails. His velvet antlers glowed in the sun.

The next day Frank joined our wanderings. At Dean's again for breakfast, we imbibed more of his locally-flavored stories. "The Polish were from the wrong side of the tracks, the Wilebski's farther than that. Now we all blend together, Polish married Scandinavians, Scandinavians married Poles."

Our last afternoon, we traveled County Road 4 west and north to a town called Caribou, the caribou population now zero, the human population nearly that. But we located what we were looking for, a Ukrainian Orthodox Church glowing against the tree line along the Roseau River, the Canadian border spitting distance on the other side. The padlock on the door revealed that the church had closed in 2005 after exactly one hundred years of service. Still, the graveyard and grounds were carefully tended, the church building freshly painted, the onion dome gilded and glistening. A flock of magpies flew by to admire their reflections.

Only one critter we never did see – short-eared owls. David, non-plussed, guaranteed that the next time we visit Kittson County, we'll see "a truckload."

(Reprinted from the *Star Tribune*)

Warbler Day Birding Report
(May 2016)

Many of us have backyard bird feeders, and delight in luring hungry nature to our city realm. This spring we have greeted customary returnees – songster house finches, bright gold-finches, the solitary brown creeper – plus our first ever rose-breasted grosbeak and a loud wren couple noisily nesting in our birch bark birdhouse. Meanwhile the American robin, *turdus migratorius,* serenades the neighborhood from bou-levard branches, its liquid thrush song complementing the sexy whistles of the year-round resident cardinals.

But at least once a year, it's worthwhile to visit the birds where they live on their own.

May twelfth is Spring Warbler Day this year, when a small flock of humans welcomes spring migrants and cheers their sound and light show.

The weather this May date was not propitious. After some summer-like eighties weeks ago, a cold Canadian kiss puckered Minnesotan lips. Still, five intrepid birders gripped the weather challenge in our talons and were rewarded.

At five a.m. we gathered at the Perkins restaurant in Hastings for eggs, toast, coffee and conversation with our birding guru, naturalist David Astin. A sweet honey bear of a man, Dave seems to know the stories of most living things. David had taken on the mantle of Warbler Day organizer from Chip Longacre, former neighbor who began these modern treks thirty years prior, following the birding route pioneered by Thomas Sadler Roberts (1858-1947), Minne-apolis physician and self-taught ornithologist who became the first professor of ornithology at the University of Minnesota. We departed Perkins at 6am for Welch Village on the Cannon River, following Robert's route and David's car like ducklings.

Dawn in the Cannon River valley bloomed suddenly clear, illuminating every emerging leaf in a bath of molten gold. The valley looked and sounded like Times Square at high noon. We saw and heard a loud chorus of rose-breasted grosbeaks, northern orioles, a rufous-sided towhee in full head-tilted whistle, flitting pairs of yellow warblers, and blackburnian warblers with striking orange-gold-black bodies. All showed off for us (and prospective mates) in glorious light, a dawn chorus especially resonant inside the concert hall of the valley.

At nearby Bell's Creek, which flows into the Cannon, two silent pair of Canada geese waited serenely as we human intruders filled our eyes and ears with more yellow warblers, goldfinches and sprays of native sparrows and swallows, accompanied by the dazzling solo of a male catbird, our mockingbird, our Pavarotti, our Kiri Te Kanawa. These returning migrants were as ecstatic to be back in their nesting grounds as we were to see and hear them.

We continued down the Robert's trail to Old Frontenac, but a spit of nasty cold north wind blew us and the birds away. Next year we will return to Frontenac, and the next, seeking green herons in the wetlands, bobolinks and bluebirds in the fields, kinglets in the cemetery, a picnic and nap in the grass, and in the woody slough along the St Croix River, the red-headed woodpecker and prothonotary warbler, where white pelicans soar along the shore.

Without Frontenac, we saw and heard 56 species this day, according to David's count, data he relayed as citizen scientist to the Laboratory of Ornithology at Cornell University, fewer than normal given the unusual cold. That's the science. The poetry came from the greening of the season – song, color, golden light, and grizzled birders filled with praise the for the springing beauty of the earth.

~~~

My "Unintentional Community," and Yours
(July 2016)

A headline in the June 30-July13 *Southwest News* caught my eye: "Proposed policy would allow more 'intentional communities' in city." Déjà vu all over again.

My wife and I are humbled veterans of the previous outbreak of "intentional community" fever in the early Seventies. For two years we were part of a rural community farm school in western Massachusetts where I was nominally "school director." It was founded by college friends on principles of consensus decision-making, sliding scale tuition, shared work and goods, and a revived relationship with food, the land and the ecosystem (a new word to us back then), Native American history and practices, cooperation and composting, recycling, green energy and more. Good ideas, mostly.

But "intentional community" proved in practice a Gordian knot of maddening governance complexity that drove my practical wife batty (not to mention the manure floating in the milk pail and other wonders of questionable sanitation). Hard enough in a family setting to make sure the right person does the dishes not to mention make bigger decisions, never mind a group of thirty individuals of various personalities, commitments, manias, depressions, distractions and hostilities, all of which were regularly on exhibit. I remained in idealistic fog longer than Susan did, as the school prospered, but finally we moved on after two years, to discover our current "unintentional community," which we call "neighborhood."

America's history of "intentional communities" holds several lessons for our current crop of newbies. Utopian Brook Farm was founded in 1841 by idealistic Emersonian Transcendentalists (though not Emerson himself). A few miles outside of Boston, this famous experiment in intentional community and self-sufficiency soon became a famous flop. Nathaniel Hawthorne, an initial though always skeptical member, resigned early, writing, "even my Custom House experience was not such a thralldom and weariness; my mind and heart were freer..... Thank God, my soul is not utterly buried under a dung-heap." From our two years of experience, we echo Hawthorne's sentiments. Though our "intentional" time produced many laudable accomplishments and friendships, some life long, governance by consensus proved a nightmare.

On the other hand, the Amana Colonies of rural Iowa, founded circa 1855, became famously successful, held together for over eighty years by the glue of shared religious commitment. Shaker colonies the same, until, due to their requirement of celibacy, shall we say, the membership petered out.

A rare success story among the thousands of rural and urban communal experiments of the 1970s like ours, "The Farm" is the most famous. It was founded in rural Tennessee in 1971 by charismatic leader Stephen Gaskin and three hundred or so colorful San Francisco exiles. Read the story of the epic growing pains on Wiki, such as total lack of any understanding of infrastructure, sanitation, or farming. But unlike most communes that collapsed under the weight of idealism married to zero practical skills, like Brook Farm, Gaskin's charisma and commitment helped it survive while remaining committed to good works in the world.

So "intentional communities" are not necessarily

doomed, and I certainly wish success for this new crop of idealistic, deeply green advocates.

But for my family, after leaving our chaotic "intentional community," we discovered real community in 'neighborhood," what I now call "unintentional community." Neighborhoods are where inhabitants voluntarily rub up against each other, shoulder to shoulder, taking on the many tasks required that make a living place a community. The volunteer-run Hill and Lake Press is one example, as are the vigorous neighborhood organizations and political, social, educational and cultural groups that support community at every turn but are always voluntary, never "intentional." In Minneapolis we discovered "neighborhood," for us the right way to live and grow and prosper in community.

Thanksgiving with Misgivings
(October 2016)

How did it become so difficult to bring a family together for Thanksgiving, when the job, the purpose, the hope of the day is simply gratitude for the fall harvest with one's family?

All that's required is to roast a turkey, discuss the giblets, debate the stuffing, mash the potatoes sweet and white, pudding the corn, burn the corn bread, clean the beans, smoke the ham, whisk the gravy, make the dressing, warm the plates, un-can the cranberries, melt the butter, find the napkins, select the wine, set the table, assemble the crib, unfold the chairs, and for the vegetarian and vegan health aficionados, massage the kale.

And while waiting for the turkey to brown, go for a hike, play street football, dish gossip, sing the family song, drink the family grog, recite the family poem. What could be so hard about that?

I'll tell you how hard it has become.

All of our children now live Out West, an accident of jobs and spouses. So we now plan Thanksgiving gatherings only every other year at my sister's house in Utah, where she moved for her husband's business decades ago. Utah? Do the Mormons even celebrate Thanksgiving? Don't they just conduct plural marriages, knock on doors, prosper in business, and grow presidential candidates?

Of course we have to fly there, flapping our wings and offsetting our carbon emissions, both exhausting. Other family members drive, four from New Mexico, one "grandbaby" from college, another with her new driver's license, tearing themselves away from friends to trek over the mountains.

But Utah's attractions turn out to be huge, and I don't mean just the mountains and sky. My sister is the Perle Mesta of the west. And her daughter runs a successful gourmet cooking school in San Francisco, and, insanely, *loves to get up early to cook on her day off!* Another niece, who lives in Park City, inherited her family's super-organizational gene, so the day will be full and fun. Finally, get this, my sister's son just got hired as a sommelier in Sonoma! Meaning there will be serious wine, not whining, this Thanksgiving!

Still, after two years of planning, the following details remain unresolved as I write this one week before departure.

1) Our SoCal kids now will not make it, the baby grandson deemed too new to travel.

2) My sister's bathroom rehab, needed to accommodate the Thanksgiving throng, remains under construction. Yes, the contractor guaranteed completion by Thanksgiving, now possibly by Christmas. Meanwhile, she backed her car into the dumpster in the driveway, the bumper now affixed with

duct tape. The dinner plates, are they under the sawdust pile or just coated with it? Don't worry that the new bathroom doesn't have a shower curtain, it doesn't have a shower either, or a mirror to assess the damage. Where ARE the air mattresses?

How much easier were the old days. Or were they?

Every Thanksgiving my parents stuffed our family of five into Dad's dusty two-door Plymouth for the drive from De-Pere, Wisconsin, to Appleton, an interminable distance of 30 miles. How *could* a trip take so long?

To pass the time in the car, we sang show tunes. Dad's resonant baritone vibrated the windows while mother and sisters added sublime alto harmonies. Meanwhile this baby brother sat, surly and soundless, fearing a froglike croak. On arrival, dozens of unknown relatives patted me on the head while whispering to themselves, "Oh Oh, a mouth breather."

That mouth breather is now a grandfather who gently pats the heads of mysterious grandchildren who look up quizzically, "Who is this geezer?" Fortunately, most do not run away.

Of course we all sing with gusto the old family song:

> *"Over the River and through the woods,*
> *to Grandmother's house we go.*
> *The horse knows the way, to carry the sleigh,*
> *through the white and drifted snow."*

Wait? "White and drifted snow?" This is a Christmas song! But my sister and I clearly remember snow always by Thanksgiving back then, sadly rare these days. Meanwhile, bird flu just decimated the Minnesota domestic turkey population, though we are assured potatoes remain plentiful. Distance, climate change, food drought – the times they are a changing.

But Thanksgiving traditions and songs limp right along: *"It's grandmother's cap I spy..."* Well, her silver tresses these days. *"Hurrah for the fun, is the pudding done...? "* Pudding? Who forgot to turn down the oven? Why did you open the tin foil? Where is the platter, the hard sauce?

"Hurrah for the pumpkin pie!" I couldn't agree more, since my job is to contribute the pumpkin pies. I employ only the old family recipe, which coincidentally happens to be printed on the back of the can of pumpkin pie filling. I do everything it says except when it comes to spices. I double them, except the cinnamon.

Happy Thanksgiving to all. If you can pull it off.

Fifty Years of Wedded Bliss
(November 2016)

As I write this, the nation is two days away from deciding to marry for four years either Hillary Clinton or... not. I have been aware of election cycles since Eisenhower-Stevenson, all of them seeming close with both political parties passionate for their candidates before the vote. But this campaign has taken on a special ugliness, more like a bitter divorce than a marriage.

So I made the decision two weeks ago to turn off the radio, not read the newspapers, work hard for my candidate and ignore the noise... by listening to a CD of Garrison Keillor's jokebook!

Which brings up wedding anniversaries, in particular Susan's and mine, fifty years this fall, which is a "true fact" both of chronological duration and pure magical astonishment. You remember the shoutouts on Prairie Home Companion for x and y, married fifty years, and everyone cheers and claps, because... What are the odds????

Because, as we know, marriage is like a deck of cards. You start out with two hearts and a diamond and end up wishing for a club and a spade!

And we all know why divorce is so expensive. Because it's worth it!

As a comfort to both of us in this extremity, we bought two plush teddy bears so we can both have someone soft and snuggly to sleep with!

At 50 years of marriage, Susan and I have achieved a nearly perfect balance – we disagree on practically everything! Except, it turns out, politics, the planet, women's rights, the glories of our children and grandchildren, the necessary warmth and comfort of friends, and the embrace of the neighborhood which has made our past four decades impossibly settled, square, active, accessible and joyful.

So in celebration, we have agreed to host a party that follows the practice of the cannibals. What do cannibals do at a wedding? Toast the bride and groom, of course! We'll toast our fiftieth anniversary as well.

May you all experience the flames we have - fiery passion, warmth in the night, companionship by day, division of labor and shared responsibilities, burning disagreements, occasional hot anger, and always the cool common sense that we are insanely lucky to have found each other, to still be together, that every time we reached for the club and the spade we remembered in time two hearts and a diamond.

People ask us if we are happily married. Of course, we respond. Every week we go to a romantic restaurant, have a candlelit dinner, delicious food and wine, and contemplate our happiness. She goes Fridays, I go Tuesdays!

But when times are important, we go together.

Fifty Years Of Wedded Bliss, Take 2

(December 2016)

Last month in this space, under the spell of the questionable taste of Garrison Keillor marriage jokes, I told a version of the truth about my fifty years of wedded bliss. This month I'll tell another.

That I don't understand love and marriage any better now than I did on that day fifty-two years ago when I danced with a woman I had never met before, and we are still dancing.

Can you explain?

My wife and I just spent Thanksgiving with our son and daughter-in-law and their two sublime babies, and our daughter-in-law told of the moment that she walked by our son in the Los Angeles bar where he worked, and suddenly leapt into his arms. They whirled twice around the dance floor, then he went back to work and she went home. The next morning she told a friend: "I fell in love last night." And so did he.

Can you explain?

In last month's column I gave the impression that fifty years of marriage may have some edges, even hard, difficult, nearly impossible edges. All true. That's why for many it takes more than one marriage, not to mention one "relationship" in today's parlance, to get it right. But for us, we both knew right away. But how? Why?

No idea. None. Nada. Zero. Zip. Pure astonishment.

We danced our way out of a noisy college party 52 years ago and landed in Minneapolis forty-two years ago, and right now I'm in the kitchen on the corner of Girard and Lincoln, she sleeping upstairs after a long night dancing with her beloved MacBook Air, now in the pre-dawn dark I'm dancing with coffee and my beloved MacBook Air, where this impossible love story tumbles out before me and now you.

A true love story, today including four adult children and eight grandchildren scattered across the landscape, all sublime, all with edges, plus countless neighbors and friends and colleagues and family supporting us along the way, many living in this neighborhood in this golden milling city on the Mississippi. After fifty years of marriage, my cup runneth over, moonlight dancing silver across the kitchen floor.

❦

Happy Holidays from Monster Trucks and Book Arts
(January 2017)

This morning, December eleventh, eight inches of fluffy new snow exalts the neighborhood. I sent photos of it as hopeful messages to the outside world that winter still exists, at least in Minnesota, at least for a few more years.

Last night as the snow began to fall in earnest, I set out to attend the release party for the Winter Book at Minnesota Center for Book Arts [MCBA] in the Open Book center downtown. Kenwood neighbor and friend Heid Erdrich is to be the star of the show this year, the poet whose text was chosen to inspire artistic fire among the cadre of book artists designing, printing and binding a limited-edition work of art you can hold in your hands.

I am an unabashed member of this "tiniest lunatic fringe in America," as artist Leonard Baskin once mused about those who love books in every imaginable physical form.

I visit MCBA regularly and served on the board for many years.

The drive from my house at the corner of Girard and Lincoln to MCBA's home in Open Book usually takes ten minutes. Last night it took thirty. Washington Avenue was gridlocked. What is going on? Have Minnesotans lost their ability to drive in snow during our long wait for winter?

As I idled on Chicago Avenue waiting to access colluded Washington Avenue, I watched a thick stream of families – fathers holding the hands of children – hustling from parking lots toward downtown. How wonderful, I thought, families attending the Book Arts celebration or the Hollidazzle parade! But wait? Hollidazzle has moved to Loring Park! What other compelling entertainment could be pulling families downtown in a near blizzard?

Then I recalled the blaring TV ads showing pickup trucks with roll bars and six-foot balloon tires flipping over each other in roars of horsepower and exhaust. "Monster Truck rally at US Bank Stadium!" Ahh! These families are not looking for the quiet beauty of books or a candlelit holiday spectacle, but dinosaur howls from the vanishing Age of Fossil-Fuels, teaching children to love those remnant bones.

My car finally bunny-hopped to Open Book in time to join a hundred others marveling as our ears, eyes, minds, hands and hearts were opened by the radiant energy of an artists' book – poems by Heid Erdrich accompanied by inspired visual art from Andrea Carlson, Jim Denomie, Aza Erdrich, Louise Erdrich, Eric Gansworth, Johnathan Thunder and Dyani White hawk, all assembled and bound by the skilled book artists at MCBA.

I love all people, from Monster Truck enthusiasts to poets and artists who make a limited-edition book that will live long after the Monster trucks are shredded for scrap. I do not love Monster Trucks. In this hopeful mid-winter whiteout, I lay my body down in the snowy embrace of the arts, to make angels for children forever to come.

My neighbor, poet Robert Bly, offers advice for monstrous times like these. Here's the last verse of his poem "Listening?"

> *The hermit said: "Because the world is mad,*
> *The only way through the world is to learn*
> *The arts and double the madness!" Are you listening?*

I'm listening. My holiday wish is that winter remain so persistent, snowy and cold that it refreshes Greenland glaciers and rebuild Arctic ice. But since that is unlikely, as monster trucks still run wild, may the rest of us "learn the arts and double the madness."

Valentine's Day: Of Dogs and Love
(February 2017)

A few years ago I finished writing this column at a Peet's coffee shop in Chicago prior to an event for my book that night. I bantered with the smiling cashier, who remembered my name when I came back for a second espresso (or was it my third?!?) I joked that I can hardly remember the names of my children, never mind their birthdays. She responded with a smile, "When my father calls me by the dog's name, I know I am loved."

I have remembered her words ever since and on this Valentine's Day I wanted you to hear them too. How understanding and generous and wise they are. "When my father calls me by the dog's name, I know I am loved."

We all know the warmth of unambiguous love offered by

the family dog. And, by implied comparison, how human-to-human love is so... complicated.

Start with dog love. The relationship with "man's best friend" stands as close to pure love as we humans will ever know. The dog will die for you rather than leave your side. Unambiguous, uncomplicated, unconflicted, undemanding, pure loyalty costing only a few handfuls of grain pellets and a short walk or two a day. In return, leaping ecstasy!

There is a genetic case for this. Dogs descend from wolves who live in hierarchical hunting packs. At the Wildlife Science Center in Stacy, Minnesota, I have observed a captive pack demonstrate the clear hierarchy of relationships. The dominant Alpha male, and sub-dominant males and females all fit in a clear order based upon periodic testing of one another. They are like Chinese society as decreed by Confucius: A loyal hierarchy from son to father to prince, in reverse a series of clear subservient loyalties.

Dog-human love began like this. Our ancestors, having learned fire and thus cooking (which makes protein more available, hence our brains grew bigger), spent millenniums around communal fires learning complex conversation and throwing remnant bones into the darkness around them. Waiting at the margin of firelight were the canid ancestors of dogs. At some point a genetic leap took place to switch loyalty from the alpha male to the alpha human. One explanation is that humans may have raised orphan wolf pups who imprinted on those who fed them. As likely, sub-dominant wolves learned over time that those creatures squatting in the firelight were a more reliable food source than that snarling, nipping, snoozing pack leader. In either case, dogs are simply sub-dominate canids who came to believe, in spite of all the evidence, that YOU are inherently dominant, a GOD! Thus they offer you pure loyalty and subservience. We call that love.

How far we human partners fall from that gold standard! Which is why there is only one dog love story, immediately recognizable, and eight billion human ones, each different. Love stories magical, complicated, conflicted, impossible, beautiful, ancient and new filled with hearts speared by Cupid and broken by Zeus and compelled by Eros and plotted by Venus and defeated by the Janus of duplicity. "How do I love thee?" Elizabeth Barrett Browning intoned in 1850 in her sublime sonnet number 43, "let me count the ways."

"All you need is Love, Love is all you need," sang the Beatles. If that were true, we'd be dogs. Instead, we have dogs to demonstrate the ideal love called loyalty. Human lovers show us that romance and complication make much more interesting stories and poems and lives over time. If you doubt, visit the booming Romance aisle in the book stalls at any airport. What is love? "Let us count the ways."

PRAYER TO SPRING

Open the door.
So many births!
A sun!

And the vernal equinox,
what is that but words
in an ancient tongue
changing everything
to tulips!

Open the door,
what is out there but the rain.
Let the floods come.
Let the warblers tread
home to their nests.

Let the worms glisten in love
under the cover of old leaves.
Let jack-the-pulpit open his
sermon with praise.

Let new words erupt:
crocus, daffodil, jonquil,
petals moving their
colorful lips.
And buds! Billions of buds!
May they burst with joy.

Let the bumblebee stumble
from her grassy cave.

And the bear with her cubs
the same.

And the spade and the plow,
let them come,
punch seed into soil,
how much good the dirt knows!

Let oak and elm unfurl
their thousand hands
to shelter with shade
the open door.

Who can stop this clapping!
This audience of everything!

You, Me, and Mother Earth
(April 2017)

With 2000 others I am off to Northrup Auditorium tonight, April 13, 2017 to listen to a presentation by Elizabeth Kolbert, the New Yorker journalist and author of the Pulitzer-Prize winning "The Sixth Extinction." It is a brilliant book though not a happy story. The fossil and geologic record detail five great extinctions of species on our home planet, the final one taking out the dinosaurs and allowing a small, wily mammal to become… us. And how we, with our big brains and opposable thumbs today propel the Sixth Great Extinction with astonishing speed, caused by fossil fuel consumption, plastic waste and short-term agricultural and forestry practices that cook the creatures of the sea and poison or torch the creatures of the land. I hate to think what she will say tonight about the Great Barrier Reef, just declared "terminal" due to the heated, acidic ocean.

Sowhadddrwegonnadoaboudit? Well, we are not going to quit.

My wife and I participated in the first Earth Day, April 22, 1970, conceived by Wisconsin Senator Gaylord Nelson on a plane back from witnessing a devastating oil spill in California's Santa Barbara Channel. His idea, taken from the anti-war movement, was to have teach-ins around the country about the effects of runaway pollution. The environmental success from that era has been broad and effective.

When I grew up in Green Bay, Wisconsin, it rained dark feathers of coal ash daily from the skies, soiling our laundry, our eyes, our lungs, our lives. Meanwhile the industrial sewer known as the Fox River ran in our back yards toxic and untouchable. All that has changed. Today the skies are over Green Bay are clear, the waters clean and safe. The environmental protection laws and policies enacted in 1970 and thereafter, often nonpartisan, saved money, species and lives.

Global Warming is the ultimate test. The fundamental science of the greenhouse effect has been clear to scientists for more than a hundred years and to the global public since 1988, when Dr. James Hansen, an Iowa boy now directing the Climate Science program at Columbia University, testified before Congress that scientists could now clearly see the fingerprints of human activity on the observed warming climate. In 1990 the United Nations Intergovernmental Panel on Climate Change assembled all the scientific facts, leading in 2015 to the historic agreement signed in Paris by 195 countries.

That global consensus for urgent action lacks only the support of America's Republican party, propped up by fossil fuel interests and politicized into denial of climate science on fact-free Fox News and the Wall Street Journal editorial pages among others. Meanwhile the Russians, whose only major business is oil and gas, helped elect Donald Trump, who paid them back by placing the worst possible climate science deniers in key government posts.

We citizens have much to do.

Start by spending political time and money in districts that elected climate science deniers; they must be voted out. Meanwhile, vote in our local reps, all leaders on climate responsiveness.

Second, on Earth Day, April 22, 2017, join the global *March for Science*. Astonishing that we need to march for *science*, humanity's greatest gift to itself, but such are the effects of these denialist times. Facts matter.

And on Saturday, April 29, join the historic *People's Climate March* everywhere on earth, including the Mall in Washington, DC. Bring banners, children, bikes, Volts, Bolts, Teslas, feet, hands, hearts and hopes. Because as my climate activist/inventor friend Dave Carroll says, "No one gets to retire until we fix this thing." This "thing" is Mother Earth with a fever, the only planet in the cosmic neighborhood where we'd ever want to live. We fixed her once. Let's do it again.

❧

A Bee-Friendly Neighborhood
(April 2017)

Over the decades, The Urban Coyote has enthusiastically chronicled the increasing variety of wildlife resident among us – opossum, raccoon, fox, deer, of course coyotes, now common; Canada geese, believe it or not once rare; egrets, great-blue herons, night herons, saw-whet and screech owls, Sharp-shinned and Cooper's hawks, bald eagles and more.

Only wolves and black bears and mountain lions and sand-hill cranes seem to have not yet found a home here (call me if you find any nesting or denning in your backyard).

In addition, a few hardy souls have kept honeybees in the neighborhood, once an illegal urban practice, honeybees classified as livestock. Today it is legal for any of us to keep bees, with the permission of our immediate neighbors, and reap the sweet reward. But tending hives, even with the knowledgeable assistance of the Bee Squad from the Bee Lab at the University of Minnesota, may prove impractical for busy human lives.

Still, there are practical steps that all property owners can take to help our bee cousins prosper. One is ending careless use of pesticides or fungicides and herbicides. A second is to create bee-friendly lawns and landscapes. The bee lab offers detailed advice and assistance on all of this. The simplest practice is to raise lawnmower cutting height to 3.5 inches or higher, allowing clover, fescues and others to continue to flower.

Last month, at Isles Studio, a magical store more like a neighborhood natural history museum, owner Jeff Bengtson generously hosted an event to benefit local honeybees, *Apis Mellifera*. I was asked to read a few poems from an anthology I edited, "If Bees Are Few," just published by University of Minnesota Press, a hive of poems about bees from Sappho to the current poet Laureate of England Carol Ann Duffy, all proceeds from sales dedicated to the Bee Lab at the University. Then honeybee entomologist Jenny Warner offered hard science and practical advice on bees, beekeeping, and bee friendly urban landscapes, then shared some of her own delicious honey.

Much more must be done, of course, to recreate habitat friendly to species other than our own, including at the corner of Girard and Lincoln, as homo sapiens reawakens to the needs of species with whom we share our neighborhood and planet. Becoming bee-friendly is a sweet place to start.

Memorial Day in Lakewood Cemetery
(May 2017)

The French lilacs have passed, the Korean lilacs bloom, and I am hanging out with the dead. It is Memorial Day, set aside to bow heavy-headed before those who have bloomed and gone. So today I am contemplating the markers, trees and people planted in Lakewood, our serene neighborhood cemetery.

My first stop is the shrine of Paul, Sheila and Marcia Wellstone, our beloved Senator and family killed in a plane crash on October 25, 2002. An engraved granite boulder marks their burial in Lakewood's northwest corner overlooking sparkling, breeze-swept Bde Mka Ska. A prior visitor has arrayed a carpet of long-stemmed white roses and red and white carnations in stately procession around the marker. Others have placed a multitude of small stones on top of the boulder, markers of those touched by the Wellstone family. I placed a flowering lilac branch over the engraved names, a laurel wreath for the Wellstone Way: "We all do better when we all do better." Then sat on a granite bench and pondered heavy granite thoughts.

Chet and Miriam Myers strolled by to pay homage to the Wellstone family while birding the Lakewood forest. We reminisced together about teaching careers past and present while melodies of Rose-breasted grosbeaks cascaded from white and bur oaks, red-winged blackbirds and robins whistled and warbled, and a brown thrasher quietly hunted the grass of a nearby unmarked grave.

Adjacent to the Wellstone boulder a sculpted granite angel guards the Pohlad family, the remarkable 56-year marriage of Carl and Eloise now passed. I noted that Carl was born the same date I was, August 23. That small town Iowa boy and WWII vet accomplished quite a bit in his 93 years. Today his family's banks, real estate ventures, bottlers, films and Minnesota Twins are still hitting it out of the park.

I wandered through a forest of other names engraved into the history of commerce in this city: Rudy Luther, Blaisdell, Rand, Wells, Gale, Hale, Washburn, Sit. A massive obelisk commemorates pioneering miller Charles A. Pillsbury, a sculpted sheaf of grain near the base. Nearby lay the marker of George Sturgis Pillsbury, 1921-2012, a worthy bearer of that powerful name. I knew him as a legislator and citizen brimming full of good ideas for our state. Next to him is the headstone of his older brother, Charles A. Pillsbury, named after the patriarch, killed in air combat over the Solomon Islands during WWII. In those days every family was called to war, every family sacrificed. Not far away, a second massive obelisk commemorates the eighteen men killed in the "great grain explosion May 2, 1878."

The center of Lakewood's park-like setting fluttered with hundreds of American flags representing veterans of America's wars, a surprising number from the Civil War, as Minnesotans were first in the Union to volunteer. According to the Minnesota Historical Society, the 24,000 Minnesota soldiers included "100 free black men, scores of American Indians, and at least one woman."

Perhaps that is why the city mothers and fathers who founded Lakewood in 1871 along a then rural lake well past the city's southern boundary of Franklin Avenue, organized it as both non-profit and non-denominational, a far-sighted commitment to openness at a time when most cemeteries in the nation accepted only those of a particular faith or race.

I passed classical mausoleums dedicated to the families Wood (Egyptian), McKnight (Greek), Fitchette (French), and the sublime eighteen-foot-tall marker of the brewing Gluek family, a gray granite Victorian maiden clutching an eternal red rose.

I passed on to the eastern section of the cemetery unfamiliar to me, stopping before an arresting Greek temple alone on a knoll. Inside the rank of Doric columns, carved over the door, are the names "Lowry • Goodrich," developers of our Lowry Hill neighborhood and builders of one of the finest street railway systems in the country, at its peak running more than forty miles from Stillwater to Lake Minnetonka. Dismantled through chicanery in the 1950's to the region's eternal regret, we are rebuilding it now at enormous expense.

Finally, I paid homage to Senator Hubert H. Humphrey, his ebullient signature etched a foot tall in gray granite, remembering the energy of the most effective senator in United States history, according to many historians, a tabernacle to his fearless commitment to civil and human rights.

Somewhere inside Lakewood is a plot named "Lenfestey." It is as yet unmarked and unoccupied, available for family and a few friends if room. It awaits the installation of the "Urban Coyote column" – a granite column with a howling coyote on top. I'd better get this column finished so I can start sculpting that one. It will take a while.

Sundays in the Park with Jim
(June 2017)

It's Sunday. Think I'll bike down to Lake of the Isles, admire the bustle, and sing. Sing? Yes, sing.

Saturday night we attended the Stephan Sondheim musical, "Sundays in the Park with George" at the Guthrie. A star is born in the voice and poise of Erin Mackey, the lead actress who sings as effortlessly as if leaning across your kitchen table, as beautifully as a dawn chorus.

"George" is George Seurat, the obsessive artist who developed the technique of combining dots of a few primary colors – cyan, magenta, yellow and black – to create the optical impression of a full palette, a technique later dubbed pointillism.

The play takes place in 1884 as George madly slaves over his massive masterpiece, "A Sunday Afternoon on the Island of La Grande Jatte." (The original hangs in the Art Institute in Chicago, well worth a visit).

So this June Sunday afternoon, I hummed music from that play as a rode my bicycle around Lake of the Isles. Wild purple irises bloomed in the reeds along the shore. Elegant waterlilies blossomed over green lily pads. Iridescent ducks swam by with multiple children dutifully following in line. Tannish people sunned in the grass. Pale people read books on benches or lounged in hammocks. Other colors picnicked, napped, strolled, walked, jogged, ran, roller-skated, biked. Some drove by with the windows open gawking at the people and the composition and the light.

The original *Isle de la Grande Jatte* is an island in the river Seine near the gates of Paris. It was opened as a park by the Duke of Orleans, expanded by Napoleon III and Baron Haussmann, and famously discovered in the last quarter of the 19th century by the impressionist painters as a great place to work.

Sondheim's musical, which premiered in 1984, is in the end a paean to art and its obsessions. It inspired me to write this paean to *Lac des Isles*, the heart of our own artistic mecca, *Paris de la Prairie*.

Minneapolis' founding mothers and fathers did so much right, nothing more important than insisting the lakes inside our city belong to the public. So today a million or more people use them annually as if they were their own lawns and beaches and paths. We can picnic on the grass, like Manet's famous nudes looking frankly at each other, or don our bustles like Seurat's women and strut the shore. Or simply lie down in our jeans and tees like Bohemians and watch the clouds and bicyclists scud by.

Minneapolis' independent park board has an election coming up, along with city elections. I will not use this space to endorse my favorite park Board candidates Jeanette Colby and Meg Forney, nor will I endorse my favorite city council candidate Lisa Goodman, even though we must note she was crucial in engineering the epic deal with the city council that saved the park board's budget for the next decade. Vote for whomever you like.

But as you wander, stroll, jog, or lounge along the shore of city lakes some Sunday afternoon this summer, keep in mind that our *Isle de la Grande Jatte* was not created by Dukes or Emperors or Barons, but by citizens, and it is citizens who must keep its colors vibrant. Makes one want to sing.

Six Heps of Summer Happiness
(July 2017)

When I was preparing to be interviewed for my new poetry collection on KFAI radio in June, I listened in on the previous interview with comedienne Paula Poundstone, whom I assume readers know from NPR'S "Wait! Wait! Don't Tell Me" where she is a humorist regular. She was talking about her newest book, "*The Totally Unscientific Study of The Search for Human Happiness.*" This is not the kind of book I normally read, but having overheard her drop-dead hilarious interview, I immediately ordered a copy from Birchbark Books. I finished reading it this morning and could not wait to tell you all about it. Not only is it of course hilarious, but also a somewhat serious self-help book for those for whom the pursuit of happiness, "guaranteed" in the Declaration of Independence, is a bit of an uphill run. Garrison Keillor loved it too, blurbing: *"The bravest and best improv comic of our time has now done the impossible and created a Work of Literature that has the wild, hairy spirit of performance about it. The whole family comes in for the price of one ticket and there's not a bad seat in the house."*

Here is her trick. Readers will not only convulse with tears of laughter on nearly every page (getting a hep of good exercise), often more than once (a second hep), but Poundstone's descriptions of her "totally unscientific" experiments are poignant and moving as she copes with her exasperations with her beloved three children, her OCD, her somewhat insane love of cats and dogs, her impecuniousness, and her wacky inherent Poundstonishness.

As she sets out to search for happiness, she quantifies

it into *heps* of happiness, followed by a *balou* of happiness, which is six heps, gained from her experiments. Her "unscientific" experiments include: hiking in the mountains with her physically impaired daughter (and bears!); trying to organize her disturbingly disorganized house; taking taekwondo classes; renting a Lamborghini for a day; hugging every stranger she encounters; plus others, all in the context of an hilarious, dysfunctional life.

You will love her humor, but also her compassion and hard-hepped wisdom. All of us could use some additional happiness, even those of us lucky enough to live in *Paris de la Prairie* where only Democrats fight it out for political supremacy and only our own Democratic disorganization stands in the way of progress. Read this book and laugh your way to at least one extra hep of happiness, and if you are lucky, a *balou*.

End of Summer Reading, Ready for a Fall
(August 2017)

As summer winds down, many of us still feel deservedly lazy, ready for a few more hot weekends around the lakes. Plus we relish the chance to steal a few more longer daylight hours before the September equinox calls us to the busy fall harvest. And this particular fall lurks around the September bend bearing all the obligations of normal life plus the racing pulse of a hefty political season.

To harvest remaining summer light to good account, yet gird your loins for the battles of fall, I recommend two books: *"Climate of Hope,"* by Michael Bloomberg and Carl Pope, and *"The Death and Life of the Great Lakes,"* by

Milwaukee journalist Dan Egan, a finalist for the 2017 Pulitzer Prize. Neither is that fictional beach read that leads you eagerly through the colorful lives of others. But both are gripping, page-turning factual accounts of our communal environmental calamities plus sensible ways to fix them.

Michael Bloomberg's name should be recognizable to all, the multi-billionaire founder of the Bloomberg media and financial data empire, Republican mayor of New York City from 2001-2013, and a forceful speaker at the Democratic national convention in 2016. Among his many quieter achievements, Bloomberg formed a consortium of 90 of the world's largest cities to combat and adapt to climate change. Carl Pope is the former executive director of the Sierra Club, who has worked most of his life addressing environmental challenges. This unlikely duo has produced the most hopeful book I know of on the climate calamity, not only by unblinkingly describing the vast dimensions of the problem but laying out a broad array of (mostly) workable solutions, many already underway around the globe.

Dan Egan's book tells, in nearly novelistic fashion, the chilling story of the destruction of the surprisingly fragile ecosystem we call the Great Lakes, what pioneers called the Sweetwater Seas. He describes the region's geological history and isolation followed by manmade disasters of the past two centuries. And I don't mean the sinking of the Edmund Fitzgerald, but invasive species small and smaller like zebra and quagga mussels, to large and larger, the potential calamity of Big Head carp. Fortunately, readers also meet the hardy scientists, ecologists, policymakers, fishermen and citizens who occasionally defeat them.

The two greatest natural assets of Minnesota are its beneficial four-season climate and its 14,000 Sweetwater Seas. Read these riveting books to learn how they have been damaged, and the policies that make it not too late to save them. Then act on that knowledge when you vote in the fall.

※

The Urban Coyote Wanders France
(Nov 2017)

Susan and I just returned from a visit with friends to Normandy and its World War II D-Day beaches. After airports and trains, we landed at the epic invasion site Omaha Beach at low tide, then took in Pointe de Hoc at high tide, where Army Rangers scaled 100-foot vertical cliffs to take out a massive Nazi gun emplacement on June 6, 1944. We visited cemeteries with regimental rows of crosses and Stars of David running to all horizons. deeply moving but less so than the photographic images of bodies fallen in heaps, held by their comrades.

A gentleman visiting from Paris asked to shake our hands, to thank us for "what we did." We were proud to be Americans that day, although of course "we" did nothing. It was heartening, given America's recent dyspeptic overseas military adventures, to read General Eisenhower's D-Day letter to the largest invasion force ever assembled: "a great and noble undertaking," he assured them. They, the country, and the world, believed him, then and now.

We stayed in the medieval town of Bayeux, where we examined at length (literally, 230 feet long) the famous Bayeux tapestry, a crude 10th century cartoon in embroidery of William the Bastard's conquering of Harold the Traitor in the Battle of Hastings in 1066, the D-Day of its day. And so ended, according to Brit environmentalist Paul Kingsnorth's recent essay, the reign of the Little Green Men, the original environmental souls of Angle-land. On behalf of my distant ancestors, the conquering Norman French, I apologize.

My second project in Bayeux involved a patisserie discovered down a narrow street from our B&B, where a spike-haired young baker served up dreams. I visited her every dawn, bearing gifts back to my family like gold, frankincense and myrrh.

Our last day in Normandy we drove down the coast in pelting rain to St. Malo, a lovely town fortressed and crenelated from myriad earlier wars, eighty percent destroyed by WWII bombing. Fully rebuilt and charming, the ancient walls overlook gorgeous sweeping beaches silvered by massive Channel tides, the setting of one of the most poetic novels of recent decades, *"All the Light We Cannot See."* On the drive back to Bayeux we passed iconic Mt. Saint-Michel on the horizon. Swarmed with tourists, it has been a bustling pilgrimage site from its birth in the 11th century, when *jongleurs* recited the epic *Chanson De Roland* and enterprising vendors touted sausages and trinkets to pilgrims passing by. Like the pilgrims, we were awestruck by the soaring spire of archangel Michael spearing Heaven above miles of glistening tidal flats.

In Paris we visited Notre-Dame de Paris, of course, where a sculpture of my beheaded namesake the apostle James holds his head in his hands over a portal. Then on to the museum devoted to sculptor Auguste Rodin, a modern god to the poet Rilke and to me. The studio and garden burst with Rodin's muscular bronze sculptures, once an artists' co-op where Rodin worked, introduced to it by Rilke. In the formal garden, between manicured topiary, stands the epic "Gates of Hell," as imposing and grievous and tortured as the gates of Heaven/Hell probably are, as we all will learn soon enough. Meanwhile our newspapers shout out the Hellish tragedies of Syria, Sudan, Niger, Yemen, Myanmar, Ukraine, North Korea, climate change and the Trump administration, their Hellish gates open around us most days. But not today. Not on Omaha Beach nor Pt. du Hoc. Nor Bayeux, St. Malo, Paris, or home, where decent November election results portend better days.

Meanwhile, we follow our art. I'm sure Rilke was thinking of Rodin when he wrote the poem below, translated by neighbor Robert Bly. The "god" he circled is possibly Rodin, devoted body and soul to art, while Rilke, like most of us, wrestled with the angel of uncertainty.

> *I live my life in growing orbits,*
> *which move out over the things of the world.*
> *Perhaps I can never achieve the last,*
> *but that will be my attempt.*
>
> *I am circling around God, around the ancient tower,*
> *and I have been circling for a thousand years.*
> *And I still don't know if I am a falcon,*
> *Or a storm, or a great song.*

Wandering the streets of Paris alone early our last morning, in search of a final benediction of croissants for the family, I found myself attracted to the portal of a church on a nearby side street. Hardly an epic tourist monument to the Virgin or St. Michael, it was on a far more humble scale. A neighborhood church. A place, I thought, where beheaded Saint James would be comfortable in the pews, and this James too. I entered and sat for a moment, holding my head in my hands.

Stray Voltage, and Maybe a Cow
(December 2017)

In November, the water pressure on the corner of Girard and Lincoln dropped suddenly in half. The copper pipe to the street, replaced only two years prior, had again mysteriously ruptured.

City workers promptly arrived and dug up the street once again to locate the leak. A burly woman helmed the backhoe as the foreman chatted with us. Then workers certified to work on underground plumbing replaced the water pipe once more and filled the hole. The friendly workers cheerfully provided me a chunk of the failed pipe to show to our electric utility. The copper was brittle, with two fingertip-sized holes eaten through it, eroded by stray electricity, like reverse electroplating. "Never seen that twice before," said one of the guys.

Dodd Demas, the God of All Electricians, set out to find the source of the stray voltage, probably an improper neutral. But not in our house, he learned.

Dodd then called Xcel, our electric utility. The next day an Xcel worker in a yellow hard-hat scaled the ancient leaning power pole behind the house and determined the power to the house connection was clean.

So Dodd called in Xcel's "stray voltage guy," expert in the field of undisciplined electrical voltage. But he was deer hunting all week, a legal and understandable absence in Minnesota. The following week he arrived to wave his magic wand following the route of our underground cable entering the house. Not the problem.

So Dodd tested our complete house and yard, determining clearly we were not the source of the problem voltage, a relief. As of this writing, the source remains unknown, possibly a streetlight link in the street, but that's a guess. No one really knows. Stray electricity wanders around until it finds an outlet, for some reason our copper pipe, says Dodd. A well-read man, he finds this conundrum Shakespearean.

Here is a detail you may find funny. The stray voltage expert mostly works in rural areas because dairy cows are known not to enter a barn for milking in its presence. My wife sensibly asked, then why not bring a cow to Girard Avenue and follow it around? So if you see a milk cow wandering neighborhood streets, don't worry, it's the real Xcel stray voltage expert on the job.

POSTSCRIPT. The source of the voltage was eventually discovered, a faulty ground of the natural gas pipeline running down the middle of Girard Avenue. The old gas line has since been replaced.

✦

Cold Enough For Ya (Almost) Superbowl?
(January 2018)

As I write this, Friday, Jan 5, the high temp for the day is minus eleven.

To one who has covered and fretted and fracked over climate change for three decades, nasty winter cold offers a double blessing. It brings out the loony naysayers who can't tell the difference between weather and climate, parading their anti-science ignorance before the public's mocking gaze. Meanwhile, hardy Minneapolitans get to joyfully don skates to glide on neighborhood lakes or Nordic skis or heavy boots to slide or stroll in the bliss of winter white.

We love our winters, sadly shorter with infrequent snow these days, as the rest of the country does not. Take my daughter-in-law, for example, a native Californian. No more need be said.

As the Superbowl descends upon Minneapolis on February 4, I am reminded of what Lee Lynch, in his amazing new book, *Amazing Minnesota*, calls "a bad PR day." That was the last time the National Football League demonstrated the questionable wisdom of hosting a Superbowl here. A photograph shows fans celebrating outside the Hubert H. Humphrey Metrodome hidden in a low cloud of condensate fog from their frozen breath! Debate all you will the merits of US Bank Stadium, which will be toasty inside, but hosting any winter playoff game here is a bad PR idea. It demonstrates two of our greatest assets, winter joy and hardiness, assets people viewing from warmer climes are unprepared to appreciate.

Unless... Unless... Dare I say this... a wildly enthusiastic hometown crowd propels the stalwart Purple and Gold finally over the goalposts to win the Superbowl!!! But we know better, don't we? Even with a LOUD crowd advantage. The Curse, of course.

My children are divided on The Curse. Most are firm believers. Never mind, they say, the missed chip shot field goal by Blair Walsh to lose the Vikes' previous playoff game against Seattle in the freezing cold of TCF Stadium. Forget also the NFL championship game in which Gary Anderson, "the most accurate field goal kicker in football," missed a chip shot at the end of regulation time against the Falcons, to whom we lost in overtime. They cite instead the last time the Vikings played New Orleans in the playoffs. The incomparable Brett Farve, heroic all day against the murderous intentions of New Orleans' poisonous defense, was driving to win the game. On his last ever Viking's play, wide open to run ten yards and place the ball down for an easy field goal to win the game, instead he suddenly, needlessly, inexplicably, maddeningly, yet sadly predictably, threw a pass right into the arms of a so-called Saint. The Curse.

Still, many Minneapolitans seem happy this playoff game is in Minneapolis. They have rented out drafty abandoned attic bedrooms for five thousand dollars a night to burly New Orleans football fans and their friends. What could possibly go wrong?

Speaking of wrong, maybe like last year we'll have another run of 60-degree temps in February, sunburn ratings replacing wind chill numbers. Then we'll win the Superbowl for sure. Two wrongs just might make a right.

Postscript. The Vikings won their playoff game here on Stephon Diggs' "miracle" catch and run for a walk-off touchdown! Of course the ebullient Vikings and their fans were crushed in the league championship game in Philadelphia. The Curse abides.

Prayer to Winter Answered
(February 2018)

Hard to feel bad that the Vikings missed our hometown Super Bowl. As a friend said after the "miracle" finish against, who else, the Saints, "They began to believe in Divine intervention. They should have remained pagans."

True enough. Pagans worship the earth. The modern Vikings worship in an ethereal $1.1 billion songbird-killing air-conditioned spaceship. When they landed on the hard green earth in Philadelphia's outdoor stadium, they buckled like wounded swans.

What then did the citizens of Minnesota get for hosting the coldest Super Bowl in history, which some of us worried would be the ultimate bad PR day for a TV-sated nation conditioned to flee winter cold like a nasty flu.

I prayed we would show the world a real northern winter, one with cold days warmed by a fleecy blanket of fresh snow under a bowl of blue sky over ice solid as steel. And how Minnesotans celebrate our winters by running into them, not away. And lo it came to pass.

I don't mean the passes in the Super Bowl, an astounding duel between Tom Brady and Nick Foles, won by the high-flying Eagles on a rare Brady incompletion, the proverbial "Hail Mary not-quite-full-of-grace" as the ball bounced away from a grasping-at-air Patriot in the end zone to end the game. This brilliant passing game was won not by miraculous Vikings backup QB Case Keenum but by miraculous Eagles backup QB Nick Foles, throwing strikes all day, a thrilling conclusion for our Philadelphia friends who stayed at our house (minus gouging rent!) to attend the game. They wept with joy and relief.

I *do* mean the dreamy feather duvet of fresh snow that fell the day before Super Bowl Sunday. Minneapolis showed the nation a truly glorious winter and how to celebrate it by zip-lining and more traditional pursuits. Such as...

The Luminaria Loppet on Lake of the Isles on Saturday, Feb 3, on ice so solid it supported ten thousand glowing visitors without a crack. Bundled delighted children wandered while adults trundled and swished. The best new ice sculpture this year was the "ice forest" growing between islands. Given our bracing "real" winter weather, unlike last February with two appalling runs of 60 degrees, the ice forest should stand until spring.

And the hilariously creative Art Shanties project on Lake Harriet. We loved the dozen faux fishing houses, creative witchery built on ice hard as granite and a blanket of glorious white snow under seamless skies and accelerating jet planes. Susan ecstatically rode a butterfly-winged bicycle around the lake. I was moved to (frozen) tears of laughter at the "Tomb of the Unknown Minnow."

My prayer to show the world a "real" Minnesota winter was answered, days cold and clear and bright and festive the entire week. Well done, Land of 10,000 frozen lakes, prayers and volunteers. We showed the world!

≈≈≈

Coyote Turns to Grave Thoughts
(March 2018)

What do McKnight, Pillsbury, Glueck, Ueland, Dunwoody, Loring, Lowry, Blaisdell, Woo, Humphrey, Wellstone, Sit and Lenfestey have in common? We all own real estate in Lakewood Cemetery. Captains of industry, pioneering suffragettes, an abundance Of Elks, doctors, lawyers, soldiers, restaurateurs, firefighters, journalists, clowns and two famous marathon dancers already inhabit the rolling park-like grounds on the shores of Bde Mka Ska, maybe someday also home to the Urban Coyote Column.

Lakewood is the city's first and most glorious sculpture park, filled with obelisks, Greek temples, a pyramid, romantic statues 20 feet tall (Pillsbury), 15 feet tall (Glueck) ten feet tall (Brown), modest sculpted lambs and humble sculpted logs and flat granite slabs. The Sit family arch and the Wellstone family boulder overlook the lake as Hubert Humphrey's eternal flame guards us all. This repository of regional history is open daily to visitors as a parking place for the body so the soul can wander without prejudice or worry about historical amnesia.

At a time when religious and racial prejudice and private ownership were the rule, Lakewood, founded in 1871 by abolitionist businessman Louis King, is nonprofit, non-denominational, non-racial. Created when our city was just four years old with but 13,000 residents, the founding board planned for a horizon that included the rainbow beliefs and hues of all of us.

Today an enlightened board of directors at Lakewood celebrates not only Memorial Day and Veteran's Day and Earth Day plus many other free events open to the public. But the parklike setting of more that 250 acres is open for glorious weddings as well as peaceful funerals, particularly in its historic Byzantine chapel whose interior mosaics shimmer with light refracted from 10 million hand-laid tiles.

Speaking of funerals, according to *Haven in the Heart of the City: The History of Lakewood Cemetery,* businessman Woo Ye Sing set a highwater mark for funerals in 1925. His service began at Westminster Church near downtown, after which the assembled mourners marched with a Chinese band to his house to gather up his soul, then on to Lakewood, interment followed by an elaborate Chinese dinner and gifts for all.

Of course, one can be interred quietly at Lakewood without granite or bronze or fanfare, in one of the many memorial parks and crypts. These days giant memorials and funerals are out of fashion, like knickers and roadsters and Chinese bands.

Nor for me. I admire the exuberant vision of the founders and Mr. Woo. Why not add another startling sculpture to Lakewood's garden, this one dedicated to the memory of the city's robust neighborhoods and the community newspapers who tells their tales? Why not a 20-foot-tall column with a howling coyote on top? – the Urban Coyote Column!

Unlikely. Still, Lakewood could tolerate one or two more general improvements. Green burial, without a concrete vault, is not yet allowed, to maintain the relatively even ground from "dents." I say just add a few shovelfuls of dirt as needed after the fact. A second improvement would be to allow bicycles to ride the roads inside. Lakewood is not a public park, instead a quiet and generous memorial park, a distinction with a clear difference. Yet, wouldn't it be simply wonderful to tour Lakewood's peaceful grounds on a bicycle? Bikers are allowed if visiting a grave. So bike in to visit me. If all goes according to plan I'll leave a marker to help you find your way.

A Blizzard So It Must Be Spring: Time for More Grave Thoughts
(April 2018)

How great that the annual March blizzard descended on the neighborhood in April again this year, just the way weather is supposed to be in our upended climate world. Sorry I had to miss it. I was out of town attending a friend's funeral. So funerals, not blizzards, are on my mind.

As the ground thaws I'm thinking again of what grave legacy one should leave behind to celebrate the good fortune of settling in such a great neighborhood in such a great city?

Years ago, I purchased a plot in Lakewood Cemetery, a rare smart real estate investment, where I plan to snuggle under the sod in the company of grass roots, tree roots, fungus mycelia, earthworms, ants and moles nests. How comfortable and friendly!

I already own my casket, er, 'basket, " the ingenious creation of my punning pal the architect, publisher and furniture designer Peter Kramer. A combined bookshelf/casket, AKA "basket." It currently stands upright in my office filled

with books. When I pass, my children are instructed to pre-
serve the books, for Heaven's sake, far more enduring than I,
then simply tip it over and hove me inside. The empty shelves
double as the casket cover. All set! Start the parade!

The rest of the funeral details are up to my somewhat
bewildered family, but I have hinted that I would not be unhappy with a cacophonous cortege of trumpeting bicyclists
and singing nuns and a N'Orleans style band marching up
Hennepin Avenue to the magnificent Lakewood chapel.
Under its stunning mosaic interior allow a dozen or more
friends and perhaps a few inebriated strangers caught up in
the moment to thunder out encomia. Don't hold back, I'm
in no hurry. When all good thoughts are exhausted, bicycle
the Basket to the gravesite and plop it in. If the occasion is
winter, sleds are fine.

As boldly announced in earlier columns, I've proposed
as grave marker a modest a 20-foot tall Corinthian column
with a howling coyote on top, boldly piercing the sky with
the Gluecks, Pillsburys and other industrial brewers and bak-
ers and bankers! Sadly, I've learned said design runs afoul of
Lakewood height restrictions for my modest family plot. So
maybe plant a white pine and a contemplative bench instead.

A second glitch, current regulations require concrete
vaults for burials to prevent "dents" in the soil as one's body
relaxes into the landscape. Dents? My car has "dents" and
looks just fine! I'll have to hold off this funeral thing until the
board passes updated "green burial" regs.

Meanwhile, spring is in the air! The ground thawed, sap
rises, mycelium moves, crocuses poke from between stones.
Time for families to visit strangers and loved ones and place
fresh flowers at the markers. When the time comes, look for
me under a "dent" in the sod. Leave me the latest copy of the
Hill and Lake Press.

Kenwood Park, Paradise Interruptus
on the Prairie
(May 2018)

How great that the traditional March blizzard landed upon the neighborhood in mid-April this year, just the way weather is supposed to act in our upended climate world (read *Climate Nexus* for the latest in terrifying global warming news). A few days after the worst of it, I walked to Birchbark Books past the north end of Lake of the Isles where I heard shrieks of joy emanating from Kenwood Park across the street. Neighborhood kids on sleds tore final runs down the park's hair-raising slopes, arguably a late spring season sledding record.

I remember discovering those slopes after we moved to the neighborhood in 1974. Every year since we hauled our children, then grandchildren to those slopes for ideal sledding (except when crashing into trees, fortunately no broken bones!).

A warm two weeks after the sledding shrieks stopped I opened my tennis gear bag at 7 a.m. at the Kenwood Park courts. I admired the freshly painted surfaces and lines, the new nets, park staff completing installation of wind screens. They helpfully pointed out the few remaining glaciers of snow and ice loitering in the shadows. The day and the courts were fine.

Around us a cacophony of bird song cascaded from barely budded trees – robins thrushing, woodpeckers hammering, jays nasaling, cardinals whistling, finches ariaing, warblers warbling, geese honking, the blue bowl of sky held aloft in the powerful arms of the park's ancient bur oaks.

What luck, I thought, that this paradise lives so near to

us. Then I remembered, our parks are not luck at all but the astonishing foresight of city mothers and fathers who believed no Minneapolis citizen should live more than a ten-block walk from a public park, one of the many reasons the Minneapolis park system regularly earns the title of #1 park system in the nation, awarded by The Trust for Public Land.

Today a few blocks from the corner of Girard and Lincoln, neighborhood children can play t-ball, Frisbee, ultimate frisbee, soccer, baseball, and that new-fangled throwing thingies game. Younger children can climb and slide and swing (our youngest daughter, age 3, memorably broke her nose on the ancient monkey bars, since replaced). Adults can walk with friends, dogs, or alone, or lie in hilltop grass, or in a portable hammock these days, surrounded by the solace of a green and pleasant land.

And where we can play tennis! God's in her heaven, all's right with the post-blizzard world!

Oops.

At 8 a.m., hideous leaf blower monsters arrived in the horizon, scouring lawns along the park's edge. Rarrrrrrrrrr, rarrrraaaaakhhh, they roared, like warring dragons feasting on peace and quiet. On and on they raged, blowing away not only vagrant leaves and grass clippings but birdsong and any sense of peace.

Which leads me to this modest policy request: *BAN these accursed noisy leaf machines!* Allow only LOW NOISE blowers in the neighborhoods. On this point I bring good news: Many low-noise models are available from our homegrown store, TARGET, and at neighborhood hardware stores. Better news, they are electric, so you or your lawn service can charge them with wind power from WINDSOURCE selected on your XCEL energy bill, leaving a zero-carbon footprint. Finally, of course, there is the humble hand rake of recent memory. I have operated mine with a pair of gardening gloves for six decades, and they leave behind only a pleasant scritch scritch scritch above the silent ahhh and relaxed grin of Mother Earth.

Silence does not exist. But stillness need not be a vagrant dream. Life in one of the remaining natural corners of the city should be allowed to sing its song without the maddening rattle of gas-hogging, soul-grating noise machines. Neighbors unite! We have nothing to lose but our earplugs, everything to gain from nature's joyous chorus.

Sebastian Joe's: Friendly Neighborhood Sweet Spot
(July 2018)

Back in the bad old days of ordinary ice cream filled with "filler," there emerged a fragrant rumor from the Mississippi riverfront of a great new flavor, raspberry chocolate chip. My family stumbled with our children down to the thriving Riverplace event center to seek it out.

Then in 1984, as if by magic, Sebastian Joe's – the fount of that remarkable flavor – opened in a storefront near the corner of Hennepin and Franklin at the entrance to the neighborhood. Just in time, as the beloved lunch counter at Burch Pharmacy had closed, and Bridgeman's ice cream café farther down Hennepin was expiring.

So the Pellitzer brothers – Tim and Mike and Todd – who had been mixing ice cream at home and at RiverPlace to a new height of perfection, leaped into our breach, and the neighborhood is much sweeter for it.

Sebastian Joe's instantly became Minneapolis' go-to place for ice cream. Apparently jealous, Linden Hills landed a second Joe's to maintain a semblance of neighborhood balance.

Many of us have a special relationship with Joe's. Mine involves good children and bad advice.

When Joe's opened in 1984, we celebrated its arrival in the pages of the *Hill and Lake Press*. In gratitude, the brothers happily sponsored our first neighborhood festival, and every festival thereafter, providing free ice cream. And when, soon enough, the brothers needed counter help, our eldest son Jamie, now 51, then 14, became their first outside employee. Since then the rest of our four children worked their first jobs at Seb Joe's, slinging malted vanilla, Pavarotti, chocolate coyote and other experiments in iced divinity, along with the always sublime raspberry chocolate chip, to the throngs lined up on summer days and evenings or mainlining espresso at 6:00 a.m.

Today countless other kids have scooped ice cream and hissed espresso behind the Pellitzer's friendly counter, along with a rainbow of student and immigrant workers from around the world.

Over the years the Pellitzers bought the building and expanded around the dry cleaners on the corner to enhance the communal experience, and installed coffee roasting ovens. Today one can relax with the latest *Hill and Lake Press* along with the *Star Tribune* and *New York Times*, or work away with wifi while immersed in the fragrance of fresh coffee, croissants and ice cream.

Aside from my children, my gift to the Pellitzers was bad advice. Famous for their ice cream and now their coffee, I suggested to Tim, or was it Mike, or Todd, that they add soup to attract a noontime crowd. After a few years of badgering they tried it.

Turns out people don't go to Joe's for soup.* They go for morning coffee and fresh baked goods, midday wifi, afternoon and evening ice cream. That's more than enough perfection to fill neighborhood days with praise.

Finally, it must be said, the Pellitzer brothers may be the nicest people you will ever meet. Stop in and say hello to Mike, or is it Tim? (Todd married and decamped to Thailand or Brazil or Ecuador). Drink in their wide, sweet smiles, their kindness, their generosity, their success.

*Turns out maybe they do. Soup is back!

※

Where There's Smoke There's Climate Fire
(August 2018)

Anyone having trouble breathing? Eighteen California wildfires, the most ferocious in the state's history, plus wildfires in Utah, Montana and elsewhere in the West, are casting a pall over the rest of the United States, particularly the Dakotas, Minnesota and Michigan, and over much of the Northern hemisphere when joined by the epic wildfires in Portugal, Greece and (frighteningly) above the Arctic Circle in Sweden and Russia!

These calamities offer us spectacular sunrises and sunsets and hazy, hot days, and this terrifying neighborhood angle. A friend and former neighborhood resident who teaches art on a Greek island every summer miraculously survived a wildfire there that burst like a bomb over her island. As reported in a Greek newspaper, she raced to the ocean and swam out behind rocks as she tried to breathe under a thick blanket of acrid smoke while avoiding the fiery debris sizzling down around her, cars exploding like bombs on the cliffs above.

Why should we care, aside from the fate of distant friends and family and local asthma attacks and other annoyances?

Because our home planet is on fire and we know why — an increasingly hotter planet mostly due to the burning of fossil fuels and because another fiery election season is upon us.

When you read this, the results of the contested primaries will be known, and voter attention turned toward the general election Nov. 6. I do not know who will be on the ballot in our congressional district, nor for statewide offices, but here's what I do know.

This choices on the ballot are clear – between candidates who will continue Minnesota's far-sighted response to a fiery future, and those who will not. Those far-sighted candidates are Democrats. This is not because Republicans are ignorant of the terrifying facts of climate change and its causes, but because their party, locally and nationally, is intimidated by the vast financial and political resources of David and Charles Koch, owners of an oil and gas and pipeline behemoth based in Kansas, who are willing to spend unlimited sums on local and national races, including Minnesota's, to intimidate Republicans as well as defeat Democrats. If Republican candidates stray from the party line that denies human cause for our radically changing climate, they will find a well-funded Republican primary candidate who toes the denial line. This calamity of Republican denialism includes all three current Minnesota congressional Republicans.

That attack on climate science by oil-fueled ideological conservatives now includes attacks on scientists who practice it, including death threats, and on science itself. Consider the appalling fact that few national Republican presidential candidates dare speak even in favor of *evolution*, never mind climate science.

As smoke burns Midwestern eyes, Midwesterners must take to the polls with fire in our belies for climate hope and climate justice and climate jobs, speaking climate truth to fossil-fueled power on November 6. Voters must put out, once and for all, the fires of anti-climate science and climate change inaction. This year that means voting solely for Democrats, top to bottom of the ballot, unless some heroic Republican surfaces who bucks cowed party orthodoxy to tell the truth and act on it.

Atmospheric physics and chemistry are non-partisan. Sadly for our children and grandchildren, Republican and Democrat, modern Republicans have made climate science partisan, so only Democrats can be trusted to respect science's findings and support reasonable policy conclusions. The smoke of climate fire is everywhere upon us, the time for denial and inaction over for good.

Memo to Local Turkey: Thanksgiving Only Two Months Away
(September 2018)

We have several new neighbors near the corner of Girard and Lincoln, generally a happy occasion. Numerous construction bins are sure signs of home improvements. But not all new neighbors are leaving a happy impression. Consider our newest, a "wild" turkey.

I remember the tracks of massive prehistoric feet up the sidewalk the day after the terrible April blizzard. The three-toed dinosaur tread marched one after another straight up Girard Avenue like a confident door to door salesman. Or a serial killer. Where could this mythological beast be headed?

Where *Meleagris gallopavo* lived for the balance of the spring remains unknown. But in late summer he arrived at our back yard, which he now inhabits every day dominating the scrum under the bird feeder for dropped birdseed.

The problem with this turkey is overweening self-confidence. It believes it is the lord of its domain, in this case our backyard. If cats, dogs or squirrels approach, it scares them away with a primitive and nasty display of aggressiveness. If *homo sapiens* approaches, the same!

We are right to be wary, previously schooled in wild turkey behavior. On a biking trip in Southeastern Minnesota one June, my leg was bum-rushed by a female intent on killing my ankle, calf, and if lucky, the rest of me. We take no chances with this prehistoric monster.

Pause for a moment to consider its pedigree. When my pale and trembling ancestors arrived at Plymouth Colony in 1620 (a questionable genealogy), they immediately set about starving to death. But the local Wampanoag demonstrated not only friendliness but a variety of agricultural and culinary innovations they were happy to share (just as indigenous chef Sean Sherman and neighbor Beth Dooley will do if you buy their cookbook, *The Sioux Chef's Indigenous Kitchen*).

A major "New World "culinary discovery was the turkey, well domesticated by the locals. Flash forward to 2018 and the state of Minnesota is the largest producer of domestic turkeys in these formerly United States. The turkeys we city people know and love arrive before us plump and plucked and browned, about a foot tall when supine on the platter, a generous dinner companion. But those giant white breasts are NOT the guy parading around our back yard. This fellow, huge and arrogant in his frankly elegant iridescent feather coat, is a shameless omnivore who will attack and eat anything, including, we suspect, human flesh.

As I approached my door recently, he flew up, claws out, looked me eye to eye from his hideous "Alien" face, and squawked, "*I WANT TO DRINK YOUR BLOOD!*" I squawked back, "*I WANT TO ROAST YOUR FLESH!*" An ugly standoff.

Who will win this battle of neighborhood titans? Will Monster Tom succeed in tripping me to the turf and pecking out my eyeballs and clawing out my vitals before tearing out my jugular in a fountain of blood?

Or will this six-foot, 185-pound 74-year-old equally omnivorous and disagreeable *homo sapiens,* armed with fire poker, kitchen knife, twine and prehensile thumbs, throttle him by the neck and twist him in the air like a Chinese kite before dressing him for Thanksgiving dinner?

Tune in two months from now for the grisly conclusion to this bloodthirsty tale. One way or another, guest or feast, the turkey is attending our Thanksgiving dinner.

❧

A Truly Scary Halloween
(October 2018)

Every October thirty-first I terrify numerous dozens of trick-or-treaters who arrive at our front door at the corner of Girard and Lincoln by requiring them to undergo "The Coyote Challenge." By now most kids and parents in the neighborhood know the drill and excitedly prepare to test their courage against the urban coyote's howling jaws, though new ones arrive doubtful.

I appear at the door in a coyote-skin headdress, flashlight flashing on my spooky white beard, and ask the startled supplicants what it is they seek? "Uhh, candy," seems to be the general response. I respond that I do not GIVE candy here, they have to EARN it by demonstrating COURAGE! Do they dare undergo the COYOTE CHALLENGE?

At which point I usher those what haven't run away into the hall to face three daunting tests. To wit:

1. Remove a peanut butter cup from the jaws of my howl-ing coyote, a stuffed roadkill, gift from a naturalist friend.

2. If they dare, remove a Snickers bar from one of the five hands attached to the five arms of Bear Woman sitting in a dark corner (a bear skin blanket swaddling limbs of salvaged department store mannikins).

3. For the final and most terrifying test, I lift them to face in the hall mirror, above a broken headless statue of Bill Shakespeare … *their own scary face!!!*

4. To these traditional Stations of Scary, this year I'm add-ing a fourth: The Trap Door of Truth.

If a visitor dares wear a D… T… mask and repeats anything at the door that is untrue, a vat of hot tomato soup will fall from the sky. If he spouts one more slur on immigrants or women, a vat of pig intestines. Any coddle of dictators, a witch's brew of bison bile on his head!

Here's a better idea. I'll greet him at the door with an OBAMA mask! He HATES Obama!!!! Imagine, a BLACK man as President??? And an uppity one at that, who dared crack a joke about him at the National Press Club annual dinner?!? So the monstrous D… T… set out to dismantle everything Obama ever did, Gargantua unable to stop gorg-ing himself until he devours the entire US government!

Ahh, but I have the antidote to the D… T… masked as-sault on facts, government, fairness and reason. You do too. It's called the BALLOT !!! on Nov. 6! Satisfying as are the Urban Coyote's remedies for the D… T… reign of error, none will be as delicious as Democrats sweeping the mid-term elections on November 6th and taking control of the House to finally place some brakes on his fact-free America. Winning control of the Senate, unlikely as that is, would be even better.

Because if there is one mask scarier than a D… T… mask, it's a M…. Mc….. mask! Aieeeeee!!!!! Covered in Kentucky coal dust, exhaling air pollution, dripping acid rain into streams and rivers, this monster's vile breath alters the composition of the atmosphere! From his home in the Kentucky Underworld he abandons Senate rules and respect for science, economics and math. Such a sight at the door is too scary to contemplate. But just in case, I will build a trap door under my porch light. And if a M…. McC……. or D….. T….mask appears demanding my country abandon not only women and children and voting rights and the economy (think $1.5 trillion of added debt to finance stock buy backs for their friends) and the earth, I'll pull the trap door and send them back from whence they arose, the right hands of Beelzebub himself.

Let's hope this Halloween is not marred by such unspeakable horrors. Then I can entertain with joy the usual gaggle of witches, princes, astronauts, pirates, ninja warriors, and brides, all Forces for Good in the War for the Future. And on Nov 6 we can all cast our ballots for a post-D… T… Future of happy children and a smiling and pleasant Mother Earth.

Mid-Term Election Howl of Approval
(November 2018)

There is a lot of happy talk about all the women elected around the country in the 2018 midterms. I agree, and about time, including two female senators to represent Minnesota, a record that never again need be broken. But let's not get too gender excited. I have had the unfortunate experience of lobbying then US Representative, now newly elected US

Senator from Tennessee Marsha Blackburn. I asked her to consider supporting something – anything! – to limit the unfolding calamity of climate change. That conversation did not go well. Her politics are antediluvian, AKA Trumpian, and wearing a skirt does not help that one bit.

Though most "firsts" definitely do right by the Liberty Bell. We are proud that our 5th Congressional District was the first to send a Muslim to Congress, and now the first to send a head-scarf covered Somali-American Muslim, Ilhan Omar. Although she has yet to show legislative gifts, sometimes breaking a barrier is more than enough for a start, when we local voters know she is basically on the right side of the issues.

But for my money, the biggest news of the election is Hennepin County electing the first openly gay sheriff. And not just because David "Hutch" Hutchinson is a physically big man.

I am old enough to remember when police arrested with gusto gay men for the high crime of… seeking love with one other. Now there's a gay sheriff in town! So look out, homophobes, you gonna have to hang up your spurs and slurs, or sheriff "Hutch" gonna shut your ugly party down. Come out of the closet, other gay sheriffs! Let's make this election the beginning of a trend!

HLP's alternative energy dynamo state Rep. Frank Hornstein prevailed in a predictable landslide, 86% of the vote, foretelling more far-sighted green energy legislation coming from the House next session, encouraged along by our effective senator Scott Dibble, not on the ballot this cycle.

And our superb Hennepin County Commish Marion Greene prevailed handily. Thank Heavens, as the county's multi-billion-dollar budget needs her head for figures more than ever since seasoned commissioner Peter McLaughlin was defeated.

Generous city voters again opened their wallets to support two school funding excess levy referenda to bolster the Minneapolis district budget, struggling with waves of immigrant students and the needs of students living in deep poverty. Kudos to voters who care for all children's education when so many are being left behind around the country.

An important state victory was Secretary of State Steve Simon. Minnesota again ranked number one in the nation in voter turnout, as Simon's losing opponent and much of the Republican Party is shamelessly aligned with voter suppression. Not on Steve's watch, thanks to fair-minded Minnesota voters.

U.S. Rep. Keith Ellison won the race for Attorney General, which had been a worry. We were not enthralled that he abandoned our district's safe seat in the roiling ocean of Washington, where he was a forceful voice. But he will be a superb and energetic AG for two reasons. Keith is a maven for civil rights, and he will not bend the rules to exclude some citizens. His opponent, Doug Wardlow, an overt homophobe, should grab his tattered saddle and ride out of town quick to avoid arrest by the new sheriff. I am very glad the charges of abuse against Keith, which derailed the sterling career of senator Al Franken, rang as hollow to Minnesota voters as they did to the people who know the people involved best. The state and nation still reel from the loss of Franken under similar circumstances, one of the nation's most effective senators and spokesmen. It's good to remind ourselves that it was not Minnesota voters that rushed to wrong judgement based on a right-wing hit job against Franken timed to the me-too hysteria gripping national Democrats.

Fortunately, the state's electorate now offers Washington the Amy Klobuchar and Tina Smith show, two of the brightest bulbs in the US Capitol's chandelier. Both of them campaigned on "getting things done across the aisle." What a radical platform!

They will bring dignity to the partisan cauldron that is the US Senate under Devil Incarnate Mitch McConnell, where the Party of Trump now holds an even larger majority, thanks to Koch Brothers oil money plus partisan propaganda from Fox News, Sinclair Broadcasting, the National Enquirer, and voter suppression happily sanctioned by the current Supreme Court. The Senate's main game the next two years will be to try to shield from public view their Emperor's naked mendacity, election collusion, illegal backroom deals and toilet talk. Thanks to voters in House districts around the country, a huge national majority, they will not succeed, in spite of Trump's recent sacking of his nearly spineless AG Jeff Sessions in favor of a man with no spine at all.

The true heroes in this election, therefore, are voters! Let's hear it for the hometown electorate! Hip, hip, whew!

Holiday Turkey Conundrum
(December 2018)

No, I am NOT talking about President (REDACTED), our favorite Conspirator-in-Chief about whom this holiday season offers rejoicing as we watch him slow roast in his own impeachment juices, a delicious swan song for his Presidency. Nor am I referring to Santa Claus, increasingly a harbinger of overstuffed consumerism. I refer instead to our steadfast new neighbor, the "wild" turkey.

When I first chronicled its arrival under the back-yard bird feeder last September, I wrote I had hoped to invite it to Thanksgiving dinner… on a platter! A sneaky backhand grip on the neck, a few spins over the head, and voila, dinner plus several feather fans and maybe a pillow. As it grew larger,

I thought perhaps a crossbow shot to the heart, if it had a heart (and I had a crossbow).

Turns out the heart was mine. For as the months passed and it appeared daily outside the kitchen window, I not only looked forward to its arrival, but felt a growing affection. That scraggly, denuded head, those scaly prehistoric feet, that shamelessly iridescent strut up and down Girard avenue, initially bred contempt in me. But familiarity that can breed contempt can apparently also breed affection. These days I see those eyes, beady and alien, as glossy and soulful. As one of those eyes peers deeply at me through our back-door glass, I wonder, could it be love?

What the turkey actually loves, of course, is food, and our backyard is splashed with an abundance of seeds from my wife's complex of bird feeders, thanks to the piggish immigrant English sparrows that greedily spill everything. Our Native American turkey cleans up after them.

It turns out my growing turkey affection is the neighborhood exception, not the rule. Whenever I show off iPhone photos of handsome Tom peering into the kitchen through the back-door glass, friends respond with horror stories of yards being overrun! They shriek to me tales of shooing gangs of obnoxious invasives with rakes and curses toward nearby parks or streets.

In addition, Susan's online excursions have uncovered a devil's brew of dark turkey facts, fueling her turkey resentment just as my affection is growing. They have excellent sight and hearing, far better than humans, and, according to the National Wild Turkey Federation, can run 35 miles per hour and fly at nearly 55 miles per hour. In their pecking order, you are either a pecker or a peckee. Fearless around sub-dominant peckees, they will peck visiting grandchildren's eyes out if they don't properly kowtow. To survive such an encounter, one must make like an Alpha Turkey and wave a rake or an ax before they'll back down. Do not befriend them!

So dare I admit I look forward to Tom's daily arrival, and miss him when absent? That I have secretly fed him a handful of seed on occasion? Did I mention I have affectionately named him Turkey-Lurkey, from the beloved children's fable "Chicken Little." Further memo to neighbors – do NOT give wild animals pet names!

But wait! Not all neighbors are unhappy with turkey visitations. Ruth Bly, whose yard across the street shares Turkey-Lurkey's confident wanderings, says, "I like that kind of trouble." And the turkey situation could be worse. My friend and birding guru David Astin, who lives next door to Theodore Wirth Park, contends with as many sixty adults with poults ambling down his street some spring mornings. Sixty! With such an efflorescence of urban turkeys in our city, maybe we can we have it both ways: Turkey friends and turkey dinners too?

SEASON IV
PRAYER TO SUMMER

"Summer," those old Sanskrit
sounds, when summoned,
strum humdrum human lives
with light and heat 'til
we forget our nakedness.

We burn before the Solstice,
cheering a sun stuck so high it
cooks our backs and bubbled chests
and blistered necks and
lusty fevered dreams.

As corn's green scarves stretch
skyward, row after row, head high
by the Fourth of July, we praise
impossible! —
the neighbor's crowded field.

As sunflowers spin round and round
low quilts of hay and beans and kitchen
gardens coiled with advancing vines,
cool lakes and bays
cry out to us through waves
their deep and shallow songs.

We'll swim away the sweat of day
and say to all who sing
and to no one in particular
how rich we are
these summer days,

so full of ourselves, sun
captured for our needs.

We'll care not in these swollen hours
how far hot muscles strain,
how backs must stoop
and knees must bend
to reach those fruits and seeds
so ripe they stream down eager
chins and grow a tree
in Paradise.

Gratitude to Old Teachers
(July 2019)

As a young instructor in 1969 in the English Department at the University of Wisconsin–River Falls, just across the St. Croix River from the Twin Cities, I created a class in "American Indian Literature," one of the first in the nation as it turned out. I felt that a college located so close to Indian Country should not be silent on that heritage.

One of the many gifts that class gave me was lifelong friendships with several native students from the Lac Courte Oreilles reservation in the northern Wisconsin lake country near Hayward. Since then I have attended as often as possible the annual "Honor the Earth" powwow at LCO, always the third weekend in July, founded 46 years ago by LCO educator and activist Eddie Benton-Banai and others as the band reasserted dignity, history, language and tradition against the relentless depredations of the dominant society in which they struggled to live.

"Honor the Earth" is a traditional powwow, meaning the dancers, singers and visitors come not for a colorful dance competition with monetary prizes, but for the joy of gathering. Dance regalia is mostly in earth and feather tones, dance moves borrowed from bird and beast relatives. Band members, families and friends return annually from around the country, a homecoming, to which all are welcome. The beautiful LCO powwow grounds, surrounded by pine forest, is where I first danced to the native drum, the heartbeat of the earth, an honor dance for Veda Stone, a mentor to many tribal members and to me. And this powwow circle is where I once received a star quilt placed over my shoulders by former students Thelma Nayquonabe and Valerie Barber, a recognition I treasure though barely understood at the time.

Teaching in Michigan the past fifteen years had made attending the powwow difficult, an eight-hour ferry and car trip. But when I learned from Valerie's sister Rose that Val was being honored by the tribe this year, I cleared my schedule and, with the last-minute help of friends who offered me a place to stay along the way, made the trek to Hayward.

As I drove east on Highway 70 through the Chequamegon National Forest that Saturday morning, the sky was a low quilt of ominous cloud, the forecast rain. I did my best to urge those clouds away, but the rain fell, though it tapered to light drizzle as I parked at the pow wow grounds near the new LCO Tribal College. A friend, Sarah Balbin, an artist who lives nearby, also a friend of Val's and Thelma's, met me with an umbrella. We watched from a distance as Val regally stood under the shelter at the center of the arena wearing a white deerskin dress, Marine beret, cradling an eagle feather fan, her very large contingent of friends, family and supporters next to her.

The rain stopped, the sun burst out, and the announcer opened the powwow with Val's impressive story – her pioneering service in the Marines, recently profiled in a PBS documentary about native women in the military, her career as a teacher, her quiet leadership, her grit as a cancer survivor.

Then the announcer read a statement Val had prepared about the steps on her journey, which began with this: "My teacher, James P. Lenfestey, was surprised to find a group of native students in his class, but because of his welcome and what and how he taught, I learned never to stop questioning."

I was stunned. She and her fellow Native students were life changing gifts for me, welcoming me into a land, community and life way I admire and from which I learned so much. I had not considered all these years what they might have learned from me.

When the drum began, I joined the dance in honor of Val. I toe-heeled, toe-heeled slowly with her many supporters around the circle of grass in the surrounding forest, a music and setting that feels like home.

Later, after the Grand Entry of dancers from all over the region, in which Val carried the Marine Corps staff and banner, Val and Sarah and Rose and I sat together, fellow elders now, the sun glorious above us, and talked as the colorful dancers circled around. Val, who loves to deflect seriousness with humor, surprised me when she turned to me and stated forcefully, so that I might finally understand, that without the welcome my class offered, that first generation of native college students "might not have made it."

I was a 25-year-old teacher who believed my university ought to offer a course in American Indian literature, my faculty allowed me to offer it, and fifty years later a warm light shone down not only on Val's life but on my own.

Thank you, Val, with two master's degrees, a distinguished military and teaching career, breast cancer survivor, invitee to the White House for President Obama's inauguration, for remembering your old teacher as a step on your journey to where your feet, and mine, now dance with confidence.

A favorite poem by Robert Bly is titled "Gratitude to Old Teachers," a title I often cite when thinking of the many teachers who helped me and my children "walk upon the unwalked," a title and poem I offer to you to feel the same.

GRATITUDE TO OLD TEACHERS

When we stride or stroll across a frozen lake,
We place our feet where they have never been.
We walk upon the unwalked. But we are uneasy.
Who is down there but our old teachers?

Water that once could take no human weight –
We were students then – holds up our feet,
And goes on ahead of us for a mile.
Beneath us the teachers, and around us the stillness.

Grumpy Coyote Turns 75
(August 2019)

The Happy Birthday greetings kept rolling in, some from galaxies far far away. Thank you all. But I am DONE WITH BIRTHDAYS!!! Seventy-five is enough! *NO MORE!* OK, maybe one more, when/if I make it to 80. But I'm already tired this morning washing two dozen glasses leftover from the joyous feast my children and wife lovingly prepared for me and my friends, including the only cake I can't resist: Susan's carrot cake with cream cheese frosting. I am unashamed to report I found a cup of leftover frosting this morning and devoured it. Bliss!

But throughout the morning, as the August sun casts golden shadows over my typing fingers and illuminates my MacBook keyboard (my wife horrified to discover only recently I peek at the keys as I type!), I feel compelled to declare my truce with Time. Because, at age 75, I have but two tasks remaining on the agenda of this life. In no ranked order:

1. Love and care for my family of four children, eight grandchildren, various spouses and close friends and my community, and do for them anything they ask without question.

2. Solve the global climate crisis.

Back in the last century, I eagerly worked on several problems at once, like the rest of us, multi-taskers all. Health care reform – WHY do I keep getting pieces of mail saying, "THIS IS NOT A BILL!?!?" Racism, that's a big hairy monster. Repairing the system of phosphates and other fertilizers running of into nearby lakes, and preventing invasive species from further colonizing the same? Worthy. Supporting this community and its newspaper, of course. And, literary gods willing, publishing a few more collections of poems, because poetry is my art and, like all artists when asked why we do what we do, answer only that we cannot NOT do it, in my case almost every morning, fingertips expressing ever greater wonder and gratitude for creation.

But the climate crisis is a game changer. In fact, it is now THE ONLY GAME, the one that trumps every other because if we lose our cozy planet, we lose all the other battles too, the poor and marginalized first to be swept away. Should the American experiment in democracy collapse under the weight of the current D..... T..../Putin administration, no permanent loss, from the point of view of the fiery hot sun or the cold indifferent moon. But if you are a human with eleven active brain cells you know that a rapidly hotter earth is the #1 misery imaginable, growing toward an uninhabitable planet for us and many of our cousin species. So climate is the one problem I have energy to address before I expire.

So this column represents yet another maundering about retirement, but not retirement FROM something but FOR something – family, community, and Mother Earth as we have known her and been loved by her. To survive the climate crisis, for which I have had a horrified front row seat for 30 years as a journalist, nothing is more important, aside from family and community, than politics and science. Let's begin by joining the Global Climate Strike this September!

Gassed!
(November 2019)

Start with this: I love my furnace. Its whir and hum as the fall weather stiffens to frost makes my inside days a sweet and cozy delight. The spiderweb of natural gas pipelines that feed it from Canadian and Dakota gas wells is a 20th century industrial era marvel.

But a 21st century idiocy.

Gas pipelines are on my mind and that of other neighborhood residents because our natural gas utility, Center-Point Energy, with its subcontractor Michels Pipeline, is digging up our streets and sidewalks to replace existing gas mains and house connections with new plastic versions.

According to one of the workers I chatted with, such a replacement regime is required by state law, damn smart of our far-sighted forebears to make sure the infrastructure for transmission of explosive natural gas is up to date.

IF we were living in the last century!

But this is the century that recognized climate change! This is the century that tells us it is MAD to invest one penny in climate-changing fuels of the past now that we have evidence all around us of fossil-fuel's calamitous effects (viz raging fires in California and Australia, heat waves all over, drought the same, as glaciers collapse and sea and lake levels eat shorelines even in Minnesota). As my wife says, it's as if we are erecting new telephone poles to support land lines when the world has gone cellular.

Make no mistake, I have the utmost admiration for the hard-hatted, hard-working crews of Michels Pipeline, putting in twelve gritty hours a day in our unseasonable October and November cold, then rough patching in replacement sidewalks and curbs with asphalt until better weather in spring presumably arrives.

But today the nation should be tearing OUT gas infrastructure and installing instead high-capacity electricity transmission lines to feed electric heat pumps and water heaters and cars as well as LED lights and computers.

The heavy irony of this massive utility idiocy dawned fully upon me on September 26, the day I hosted an event at the house for award-winning Bengali novelist Amitav Ghosh. Ghosh had been a featured speaker at the Nobel Conference in nearby Northfield, Minnesota, the day before on the topic of climate change. So RainTaxi Review of Books, a smart new member of our state's remarkable literary ecosystem, arranged for him to stay an extra day to speak about his newest novel, *Gun Island,* at Grace Community Church in the neighborhood. I eagerly agreed to host a reception for him before the event.

Within the span of Ghosh's soon-to be Nobel-Prized

string of novels is his stunning book-length essay, *The Great Derangement: Climate Change and The Unthinkable*. For Ghosh the word "unthinkable" has two meanings: That what we "civilized" humans are doing to destabilize our home planet is in unthinkable. And that most of us literally can't think it – simply cannot see, imagine, believe what science and now our senses are telling us, that climate change is an existential crisis that requires changing... everything.

Arriving at the corner of Girard And Lincoln for the 5pm reception, Ghosh and guests threaded their way past a gaggle of construction machinery resting like Paleozoic reptiles quietly tethered for the evening from their anti-diluvian gas main replacement work – a scampering one-armed Deere with prominent claw, a Rube-Goldberg underground drilling Triceratops, one or two seemingly innocent but in fact vicious Bobcats, and a brontosaurus dump truck, all of them concrete evidence of an unthinking civilization replacing obsolete technology with obsolete technology.

At the door I greeted Ghosh with a painfully ironic grin, though I should have cried. A quiet, gentle man, Ghosh just smiled. What is there to say? Evidence of the Great Derangement is everywhere.

After the reception, we repaired to Grace Community Church where Ghosh read from his newest novel, *Gun Island*. Take the time this winter to read *The Great Derangement*, then *Gun Island*, illustrating how the Great Derangement plays out in real time. And in the spring let's get out our shovels and set the foundations for a thousand new solar gardens and wind machines around the state, and the transmission lines to connect them, for there is nothing more beautiful.

Tennis Anyone?
(February 2020)

When you read this, it will be late February, one or two feet of snow still covering the tennis courts in Kenwood Park for at least another month. Yet we who are slaves to the love of the game persist undaunted in our pursuits. Tennis is our yoga, our tai chi, our ballet, our marathon, our futball (soccer), our hockey, our practice, our spectator sport.

To keep up our practice year-round, we exploit the many fine indoor tennis facilities in the region until the sun angle melts the snow and the Park Board puts up the nets. My indoor tennis studio of choice is Baseline Tennis Center on the University's East Bank campus, a quick ten-minute drive from our neighborhood, with ten excellent hard courts, good lighting, no membership fees, available leagues, lessons and practice sessions for most abilities. And if you are a geezer like me there are abundant options to book courts whenever you can find a partner or three (i.e. not most weekend days, as Baseline hosts many regional and national tournaments). Did I mention NO membership fees! And a geezer rate (over 65) of $22 per hour, insanely low cost in this day and age (be very glad you are not a tennis practitioner in Manhattan!).

Still, we parsimonious tennis players eagerly anticipate the return of the FREE outdoor season. Michael Raimondi, commissioner of my Saturday Morning Tennis group (7-9am, coffee and conversation afterward), just conducted his annual poll anticipating the first Saturday we will play outdoors. Mike requires a temperature at 7am of 42 degrees F or above, snow melted from the courts, nets up, and enough morning sun to see the ball at least a bit. Opening day votes varied from late March to mid-May, Minnesota's "spring" notoriously fickle as it is. Meanwhile...

One of the many benefits of playing winters at Baseline is making the acquaintance of the University's Division 1 Men's and Women's tennis teams. Friends, they will save you a LOT of money! You can skip travel to Wimbledon, England, the French Open in Paris, the US Open in New York, or Indian Wells in the California desert, for you will NOT view notably better tennis than our men's and women's teams, recruited from all over the world.

Just yesterday, Feb 15, I watched our #1 player, Stephan Milicevic, a senior from Belgrade, Serbia, defeat the #1 player from the University of California-Santa Barbara, Joseph Gullin from Paris, France. The rest of the team prevailed as well, including #2 Vlad Lobak from Kiev, Ukraine, defeating Victor Krustev from Toronto, Canada, and my new favorite player, Slim Troost, a tall freshman sporting a man bun, from Tallinn, Estonia, who easily handled Alex Soto of Madrid, Spain.

Minnesota's #1 and #2 ranked men's players from last year's team, Matic Spec from Slovenia, and Felix Corwin from that well-known tennis powerhouse Elm Grove Village, Wisconsin, went right to the pro tour after graduation. Look for them on the Tennis Channel. Other graduates stay behind, some attending the Carlson school for international business, others the medical school, as will the #1 ranked woman this year, Russian-Canadian Tina Kreinis, or pursuing a doctorate in microbiology (Mikey Kantor, from St. Louis Park). On the women's side, I recommend watching the very exciting freshman Ekin Erctein, from Ankara, Turkey, although all the team members are outstanding players with astonishing power. Many of the men and women players are academic all-Americans as well.

My neighborhood friend Felix Phillips likes to grouse on occasion about how in the good-old-days the University tennis teams were entirely made up of in-state kids, and indeed his very handsome face smiles out from the 1955 and 1956 team photographs on the Baseline Wall of Fame clutching his wooden Jack Kramer racquet, as does that of another neighbor, Catherine Wadden Puzak, 1980-1984, Captain of the team those years. But Division 1 athletics, like business and science, is now fully global, and to compete at the top-level teams have to play the global game. The University plays that game at a very high level.

But do not despair, Minnesota tennis families. We can compete! One of the U team's stars the past 3 seasons is Jackson Allen from suburban Shakopee, who soundly trounced Joseph Rotheram of Manhattan Beach, CA on Saturday. And Minnesota's #6 player, Sebastian Vile, a freshman from Rochester, Minnesota, defeated Joshua Williams from suburban New York City.

Did I mention that viewing University matches at Baseline is FREE? And if you make a modest donation to the Baseline Club, the booster club for U of MN tennis, they even put out food for you? And send you a hand-written note of gratitude from one of the team members, mine from one of my favorite players, senior Eli Ogilvy from Mississauga, Ontario.

So, dear readers, if you are scrambling for year-round exercise, and like a bit of competition at the core, consider tennis. The tools of the trade are inexpensive – the new strings and carbon-fiber racquets are long-lasting, the service at Mike Lynn's Tennis Shop in the Miracle Mile shopping center on Excelsior Avenue is friendly (tell Mike and Mimzy I sent you), used rackets and shoes can be recycled to park programs, and used balls make great dog toys. And when you arrive at the woolly wrappings of geezerhood as I have, you can string your racquet softer, as I do, now 48 pounds, so all you need do is hobble within reach of the ball and these new racquets and strings do the rest. That's still good exercise, and a good feeling. Especially if the shot is called "in."

*

Sadly, despite robust protests and abundant offers of help, in 2021 the University discontinued the men's tennis program in a vain and minor effort at pandemic budget savings.

The Magnificent Wildersons
(February 2020)

Lowry Hill neighbor Ida-Lorraine Jules Wilderson peacefully passed away at age 86 on January 25 in her Lowry Hill home. A scion of our community, city and state, PhD psychologist, mother of four, 57-year resident of Lowry Hill, she leaves behind with her husband Frank, Jr. a powerful legacy in our state and an important story of our neighborhood that must be remembered.

After Ida-Lorraine's funeral at the Basilica of St. Mary, where she was as a fixture in nearly every capacity, and after an afternoon of relaxed conversation with the remarkable Wilderson family at the Woman's Club after the service, I interviewed Frank, with his daughter Fawn, at the family residence on James Avenue South.

How Frank and Ida-Lorraine managed to move from deeply segregated Louisiana, where the public school for African-American students in Frank's parish (county) went only to the 7th grade, to become college graduates, school teachers, PhDs and leaders at the University of Minnesota and the Minneapolis Public Schools, is an epic for another time. This is the story of what happened when they arrived here.

When Frank was offered a position at the U of MN's Educational Psychology Department, Ida-Lorraine was happy to move to Minneapolis from Ann Arbor, Michigan, where Frank had finished his doctorate and she was beginning work on hers. Not only did our state and city have a progressive reputation (think Hubert Humphrey), but she had served on Ann Arbor's committee to attract Tyrone Guthrie to build his much anticipated regional theater in that city. When instead Guthrie chose Minneapolis, she knew this city must be an outpost of culture. So in 1962 the family moved to Minneapolis with their three children and looked for a place to rent. For African-Americans, housing discrimination was a routine experience, and indeed the Wildersons found many apartments suddenly "rented" when they showed their black skin. But the owner of a home on Kenwood Parkway, an economics professor, welcomed them to rent for the year of his sabbatical, so they moved in. Fawn remembers watching the excavation for the original Guthrie Theater, on Vineland Place (next to where the Walker Art Center eventually would be built), thinking it was a swimming pool for the neighborhood!

As Frank and Ida-Lorraine settled into academic research, teaching, and psychology practice, they looked for a house to buy. "We knew better than to show our faces," Frank remembers, having had too many experiences of being suddenly turned away. So, when they saw in the paper a house for sale in the nearby 1700 block of James Ave South listed for an affordable $24,500, they jumped, but carefully. They immediately called the family on the phone, agreed to the price, and the family agreed to show them the house on a Sunday. The realtor grumbled but agreed to attend. When the Wilderson family drove up to the house, Frank remembers with a laugh how the realtor attempted to quickly hide his paperwork under his car seat. But when the front door of the house opened and the Wilderson children were greeted by the children of the owner's family, and they all ran off to play together. the owners agreed to accept the Wildersons' offer for the asking price, though the realtor did everything he could to stall the sale. The Wildersons insisted they type out a bill of sale on the spot, bringing their old Corona type-writer, noting the receipt of the down payment and the final price agreed to by all.

Still, difficulties arose. The parents of the homeowners tried to dissuade them from selling to an African-American family, going so far as to revoke helpful financing for a new business venture. But the paperwork was solid, and the first African-American family moved into this part of the city, and thus our world turned one more small notch toward fairness.

Recently Twin Cities Public Television produced a re-markable documentary, "Jim Crow of the North." Using Min-neapolis' digitized real estate deeds, researchers at the Univer-sity of Minnesota Libraries charted the growth of racial and religious restrictive covenants in Minneapolis deeds through-out the 20th Century. The covenants followed ugly racist in-cidents in the early twentieth century as African-American families bought lots to build houses in developing neighbor-hoods such as Prospect Park. News of their presence attracted virulent mobs of white neighbors mobilized to drive them out. Soon, covenants appeared on deeds in newly platted sec-tions of the city, refusing purchase or sale to any person of color, and often to Jews and other religious and ethnic mi-norities. In neighborhoods platted before such covenants were invented, such as Lowry Hill, subtler but firm racist systems operated. Think of how many families were quietly excluded prior to Frank and Ida-Lorraine breaking that barrier.

Restrictive covenants and other "red line" practices were finally rendered illegal in 1968 with passage of the Civil Rights Act, AKA the Fair Housing Act, carried in the U.S. Senate by Minnesota Senator Walter Mondale.

Frank Jr. still lives in the James Avenue house he and Ida-Lorraine bought in 1963 and where they raised their four children: Frank III, professor of African-American history at U. Cal-Irvine; Fawn, adjunct faculty at the U of MN Law School; Amy Cousins; and Wayne, classmate of our son's at Kenwood elementary school, now a familiar actor in Los Angeles.

Frank, Jr. is good-humored today about the struggles he and Ida-Lorraine had to undergo to gain housing in the neighborhood. Still, we who love this neighborhood and city must never forget this shameful chapter in our history.

Standard Sidewalks, Inc.
(April 2020)

After a nearly seventy-degree spring week, snow arrived Easter Sunday, followed by a week in the cold cellar. Still, the Monday after Easter, seven AM sharp, the trucks arrived, marked "Standard Sidewalk, Inc., founded 1888." In one week during the rollout of a vicious pandemic, the remarkable employees and supply chain of Standard Sidewalk produced fresh sidewalls and curbs before our eyes.

The sidewalks were needed because the lack of coordination among the various utilities that run our lives had led to not one but two recent sidewalk disruptions. The first was to redo the gas mains down the middle of the street and the connections under sidewalks to our houses, plus fix the sidewalks they'd disrupted.

The second was the installation of 5G transmitters. Whether you like it or not the neighborhood is sprouting brown tree-like metal trunks which will be the source of our putative 5G bliss: *The God of Streaming Everything*. Beneath the metal trunks lie the cables that connect them, laid last fall, which required tearing up the sidewalks once again to drill cable tunnels and create ports for connections. When winter closed in early, a quick patch of asphalt got us by until now.

Certain "sheltering-in-place" neighbors were not amused by the contractor's work schedule, a 7am start signaled by a piercing "beep beep beep" as trucks backed in to unload. But I was impressed. Every workday, right on time and in order, arrived...

1.   The truck with the blinking hazard signs;
2.   The truck with the wooden forms;
3.   the truck with the sand;
4.   The truck with the gravel;
5.   The truck with the ready-mixed concrete;
6.   The truck with the metal curb inserts;
7.   The truck with the black dirt;
8.   The truck with the grass seed and brooms to clean excess black dirt from the sidewalk;
9.   The truck to pick up the blinking hazard signs and move them down the block.

As many of us worry in the blooming pandemic about the health of supply chains for food and beer and toilet paper, the workers and managers at Standard Sidewalk Inc. demonstrated before our eyes and ears a comforting reliability, as if the COVID-19 spring of 2020 were just another work season.

And so the men and women, trucks and front-end loaders of Standard Sidewalk, Inc. continued their march on down Lincoln Avenue on the way to Hennepin, leaving clean new sidewalks and curbs in their purposeful wake. No wonder the company has been in business since 1888. How many other businesses can say the same?

Fourth Horseman of the Apocalypse
(May 2020)

Suddenly Minnesota and the nation are living fully Apocalyptic times as America's fourth horseman of the Apocalypse -- racism—rode hard into the burning night after the intolerable vision of the killing of George Floyd a week ago Monday. The other three horses of destruction were already loose in the land: pestilence, climate science denial, and Russian/Republican assault on democracy. This echo of the imagery from the Bible's Book of Revelation is scary, and also prophetic.

Last fall the Swedish teenager Greta Thunberg, the Joan of Arc of climate action, helped move the climate crisis to the front burner of the political season, with all Democratic aspirants for President plus House majority leader Nancy Pelosi fully committed to solutions, only the Trump administration and Senate majority leader Mitch McConnell and their obsequious minions committed to denying the evidence.

Then in February the coronavirus pandemic erupted its medical and economic volcano. Pandemic plagues have been documented since at least third century BCE Athens and the authors of Revelation knew them well. According to Ezekiel, the fourth horseman of the Apocalypse is "plague." Scientists marvel at COVID-19's humbling effects, with no group, class or country immune, the poor and elderly especially consumed. The latest research says it will threaten us, and change our behavior, for a very long time, with dire human and economic consequences.

Two of the jobs at risk in the American pandemic are poll worker and voter. Yet in April the Republican dominated Wisconsin and US Supreme courts refused to postpone a minor Wisconsin election to facilitate mail balloting. The result was more than 40 cases of coronavirus contracted among voters and poll workers. Citing the long history of Republican efforts at voter suppression, David Cole, National Legal Director of the American Civil Liberties Union, wrote recently, "in the coronavirus pandemic, Republicans may have discovered the ultimate voter suppression tactic."

President Trump and McConnell, virulent opponents of a healthy voting process, want to send to Hades Sen. Amy Klobuchar's bill assisting states with funds for the extra costs of mail-in balloting this pandemic year, a voting process already used safely in five states but more costly than traditional in-person voting. For the record, President Trump and the Supreme Court voted remotely, and a rigorous study of voter fraud over 12 years of absentee ballots unearthed 500 cases among billions of votes, "not even a rounding error."

Underneath all this festered America's and the world's original sin of slavery and racism, which exploded in the viral vision of the excruciating death of George Floyd on May 25th in Minneapolis. Massive protests erupted around our city and the world by people of all colors insisting our nation no longer abide racist slights and profiling and discrimination and inequality and state-sanctioned death.

No easy cure exists for any of these pandemics right now but begins with Revelations at the ballot box in November.

Zen and the Art of Spindle Painting
(June 2020)

Our old house has many ins and outs, many porches, many spindles. So what does one do during a social lockdown of a pandemic nature, with nights of racial rage and flame, but take up painting spindles. It is meditative work. Scrape, sand, brush, dip, paint.

I start with spindles few ever see, hidden behind the overgrown hedge of yew. Others are front and center on view to all passers-by. All desire their fresh coat. And so I meditate, head down, dip and paint, mind floating away on the wind.

Dip the brush, another spindle ahead.

The yew snags me in the back as I work spindle to spindle. Twenty percent unemployment so far in the pandemic, including some in my family. Dip and brush.

The yew and the juniper at the porch corners are overgrown, making the porch a cave of solitude. Lovely I think. The next owner will probably cut them down. Dip and paint. Helicopters overhead.

Practically a jungle, the neighborhood this spring, plentiful rain and sun, elm saplings suddenly burst to become trees. Norway maples tower over our side yard, a green blanket. The massive backyard bur oak will outlive the present residents of this house by another century or more. Today it claps its giant green paws above us, hungry for light.

Dip the brush, another spindle ahead.

The house was built in 1902, a comfortable home on a corner lot. A plain and easy wooden house to care for. And then, in the Twenties we believe, when people had extra money before they lost it in the Depression, owners whose names we do not know moved the entrance around the corner from Girard to Lincoln, added neoclassic details and two porches, each with sets of spindles. Thirty-nine years ago those spindles became ours. Dip, turn, another spindle ahead.

I wear white painter's gloves bought for the pandemic. They help clean the curved spindle surfaces and protect my hands. A mystery how my hands still end up covered with paint. I suspect my itchy nose, requiring glove removal. There is paint on my eyeglasses too. Dip, turn, another spindle.

The paint seems good quality, one coat primes and covers. A medallion on the side notes I will not be poisoned while using it. And it cleans up with water, not the volatile turpentine of my youth. I thank environmentalists and policymakers and paint formulators who got the lead out of paint. Dip, turn, one more spindle.

Fast drying too. I notice that once the coat is applied, the ants immediately walk upon it without sticking or marking. I admire ants, busily seeking and finding. The few in the way of my work I brush off the railing into the yew. Ants can fall very far without injury as they weigh practically nothing, with a durable body covering. If an ant were dropped from the Leaning Tower of Pisa, it would stroll right off. Ants will be here long after we are gone. Dip, turn, another spindle.

Not so the leaning tower of Pisa. It was built on a flawed foundation from the start. Construction was interrupted several times for wars and rebellions, then back at it. But no way to make it straight. If I were thinking metaphorically, George Floyd, this could be a lesson you leave us, unable to breathe. But I am painting spindles. Dip, turn, paint.

My friend the jumping spider arrives right in front of me, eight bright eyes and a beard like a Chinese philosopher. I nod with my brush, and we pass by.

I have developed painter's elbow, a form of tennis elbow. I can still perform the painting motion, but switch hands on occasion, as sirens run up distant streets, helicopters whir overhead.

I miss one spot or another. And a splash of white appears where it should not be. The second color will cover it. Dip, turn, another spindle.

I begin to feel elation as I paint, as if I were in the process of something... heroic. Say Ulysses sailing home on his paintbrush, a bubble of hope and pride rising in his chest. Along the way we navigate between dangerous whirlpools, Scylla and Charybdis, in the narrow Strait of Messina between Italy and Sicily, then sail on home. Nothing is a given on the hero's journey, nor in our nation's. Yet heroic, this painting of spindles.

One more array of spindles to go, and another lovely afternoon ahead. Glad I'm not flaying chickens that soar down the processing line at 175 miles per hour, I've heard.

Thinking of lunch, I recall one last week with my friend Peter the architect. We met at his warehouse office. I brought the soup. Peter takes the long view, which is beginning to make more sense as I paint. He likes to quote paleontologist Stephen Jay Gould: *The three ways of making a living in our world are well represented in plants (production), fungi (reduction), and animals (consumption). And as another nail in the coffin of our self-importance, I hasten to point out that the major circle of life runs between production and reduction. The world could get along well without the consumers.* That's us, he says.

Dip, turn, another spindle.

These wood spindles have suffered a long time, nearly a hundred years. We and others have replaced a handful along the way, toenailed in. Funny expression, "toenailed." A few more will need replacement, but this paint will hold them another year.

Maple seeds spin down around me and the ants, the spiders, the yew and fungi below, winged helicopters quieter and longer lasting than the war machines of the National Guard overhead.

Dip, turn, another spindle ahead. Another day allowed to breathe.

Soul of the City
(August 2020)

I am reading *The Soul of America* by Pulitzer-prize winning historian John Meacham. He describes the slow, painful steps from the revolutionary founding of the world's first democracy, representing some white men, through a Civil War to end chattel slavery, to the collapse of the Northern victory a decade later into vicious Southern obstructionism, then to Jim Crow, the KKK and Indian wars, to Lyndon Johnson's passage of the Voting Rights Act in August, 1965, arguably the date to finally celebrate the freedom of Southern African-Americans from institutional repression. In the many interstices during that long struggle to the Black Lives Matter eruption today, are many steps backward (think racist, anti-Semitic and homophobic red-lined jobs, mortgages and cities, including ours) and forward, including Women's Suffrage, school and housing desegregation, Gay liberation and marriage, that continue to pry open the door to full citizenship in the ownership society. IF you have the price of entry. That remains the rub.

Although a better record than most American cities, Minneapolis has a racist past, as abundantly documented in the recent TPT documentary "Jim Crow of the North," and our neighborhood was not exempt, as I documented with the story of Frank and Ida-Lorraine Wilderson breaking the color barrier in home ownership only in 1963. But today our neighborhood is a shining rainbow of homeowners and renters of all colors and backgrounds and gender attractions. Still, we have some atoning to do.

But what? Former mayor Betsy Hodges has accused Minneapolis' liberal neighborhoods of perpetuating racial injustice by encouraging Post-War downzoning to recapture neighborhoods from blight, revive city tax coffers, and not incidentally reversing suburban flight. The charge is non-sensical. Gentrification is an economic process, not racist, though it may have racial effects. The same is true of wine versus beer. Better answers are needed.

The proposed solution is up-zoning the city to allow more multi-family housing where space can be found or created by developers, as was the case in post-war years prior to zoning restrictions. For appropriate locations, yes. A good example is my Lowry Hill neighborhood, already a successful mix of single and multi-family residences.

But be careful. What our young city planners forget is that Minneapolis and St. Paul are not islands but surrounded by independent suburbs with quite different zoning and housing regulations and opportunities. Our region requires full metro-wide government, as suburbs are in fact part of one metro area, but that is a complicated problem for another day. Meanwhile, people who favor less density or need more room for raising families can easily move fifty feet across France Avenue into more accommodating communities. Once this was called white flight, much reversed in recent decades by the renewal of city neighborhoods. But if current urban chaos reigns, we could see a new flight to suburban safety.

What is clearly not productive was the decision to turn the nation's premier park system into temporary homeless housing camps. The Park Board belatedly caught on to the calamity of its own making but remains clueless about the real needs of the homeless population booming all around the country. Would that they had listened to County Commissioner Marion Greene telling about the abundant services and available housing for the homeless the county already provides.

The soul of our city, Minneapolis, is accessibility, brain-power in business, professions, universities and the arts, a superb park system, long-view planning, strong school systems, world-class facilities from the airport to museums to theaters to, yes, the Mall of America, to 5G, to abundant access to nature, to our much-maligned but in fact persistently generous infrastructure supporting poor and immigrant populations. Still, what has not been achieved is affordable housing for all, and proper mental health facilities for all.

What is the soul of the neighborhood? Community. Built on safety, communication, economic stability, social openness, access to services, and a fair-minded outlook locally and on the world.

Racism, sexism and homophobia are diseases, like Co-vid-19. Since the late Sixties our city and most neighborhoods have inoculated themselves against them, becoming welcoming and affirming to all neighbors. But only if they can afford the entry fee.

The subtitle of Meacham's book is, "The Battle for Our Better Angels." Do you see any angels, or only helicopters, flying overhead in this fraught political moment of George Floyd unrest, a pandemic, the climate crisis, and the tyranny of Trump abetted by his sidekick Beelzebub McConnell? I do. Political angels need not be perfect as people or policy-makers, nor, as Meacham reminds us, were Lincoln or FDR or Lyndon Johnson. But they acted on the right side of history, expanding civil and human rights and economic opportunity and stability. But to be effective they needed, and we still need, a Congressional majority to overwhelm obstructionism before we can deal with the madness of the moment and, as Martin Luther King said, bend the arc of the moral universe toward justice. We are not there yet.

From the Heights of Machu Picchu
(September 2020)

1n the fall of 1978 I found myself gazing down on Machu Picchu. I had been hiking the Inca Trail for days past other 14th century Inca ruins to this revelatory point. In fact, I had been on a walkabout since 1968 to learn as much as I could about the native history of the Americas, a subject utterly absent from my education in spite of the fact that I grew up near three native reservations outside of Green Bay, the Oneida, the Menominee and the Brotherton.

Settling in Minneapolis in 1974, now with three small children, we discovered Paradise – a stable, beautiful, family-friendly neighborhood in a thriving, arts-loving city in an open-hearted, open-minded, inclusive state. I taught Native American literature and further studied the history of the Native Americas I had never been taught.

Which led me to South America and the story of Conquistador Francisco Pizarro, who confronted the mighty Inca civilization, as large north to south as the Roman empire, in 1532 with 188 soldiers, guns and horses. With daring treachery, he won. His army should have been obliterated by the highly organized Incan generals, but for a mysterious pandemic. Smallpox accidentally introduced to South America by European explorers and coastal slavers worked its way inland and struck the heart of the Inca royal court in Cuzco, killing the Inca emperor and his chosen successor. That led to a fratricidal civil war of succession into the bitter shambles of which rode Pizarro with his horses and treachery and cross. That pandemic changed history.

As our beloved city and country reel from the COVID-19 pandemic of 2020, plus the calamities of racial injustice and political corruption at the top of our fragile democracy, the view of Machu Picchu rises again in my mind. My freedom and prosperity and heath care and education and environmental protection and democratic processes and luck allowed me to look down from the Inca Trail on a mysteriously abandoned sacred city carved out of living rock like sculpture.

Why am I telling you this? Because every minute is history, but some minutes are flex points, when good things or bad things come together and big change happens.

Minneapolis combines two words, the Lakota *Minne,* meaning water, and *polis,* Greek for city.

Right now our beloved water city feels instead like *terra incognita,* an unknown world over the edge of the known horizon. How will the COVID-19 pandemic play out here and around the globe? When will a vaccine arrive? How well will it protect? How will businesses survive another year, so many workers without jobs or support? Will the downtown ever recover from a Zooming workforce? Will the city recover from racial strife? Will resurgent crime and anarchy be quelled? How will our mayor and city council ensure the absolute necessity of public safety without which no neighborhood or city thrives, but also public justice and reparations? Will the 2020 election on Nov. 3 allow Gov. Tim Walz to fully succeed? And will it end the corrupt tyranny of Trump/McConnell?

Our city and country are on edge. When I look down

from above, I see *minne* and *polis,* our shining water city, divided into islands, our dis-United States at war with itself. Will visitors five hundred years hence look down upon us and dimly recall our stain of racial slavery, our theft of native lands, and how everything beautiful fell apart during a pandemic? Or how we survived and prospered, courageously facing the hard facts of our time?

Halloween in a Dr. Fauci Mask
(October 2020)

A lot of neighbors are scratching their heads about how to participate in Halloween this October 31 in the midst of pandemics political and viral. Coyote's answer to the first is obvious – VOTE by mail or in person on or by Tuesday, Nov 3. If all eligible Americans take this prophylactic step, the disease known as Trumpism will recede into an ugly asterisk in history, down there with Andrew Johnson who, after Lincoln was assassinated, attempted to undo the victory against slavery in the Civil War. But what to do about the Halloween holiday during the COVID-19 pandemic is a more complex business.

HALLOWEEN is the most democratic of celebrations, open to all, a thrill ride of American childhood filled with ghosts and goblins, mummies and witches, treats for tricks, a generous gift exchange, the happiest undead day of the year. And so much has been canceled already, while some events that should have been canceled were not, like the Vikings' season. Stay Home, Vikings! For the rest of us, that sad advice is appropriate for so much of this socially-distanced year. But the Urban Coyote refuses allow this killjoy pandemic to crush this favorite of children's holidays. Below are steps the Urban Coyote will be taking to ensure a Happy Pandemic Halloween – delicious, scary and safe. I hope all readers – children, parents and guardians – will visit, wearing Dr. Fauci masks!

I will carve pumpkins. I'll clean and dry the seeds, dredge them in oil, sprinkle with salt and chipotle powder, and place them in a moderately hot oven. Turn them several times and keep an eye out for burning. Remove and let cool, and place in a bowl. We will have a delicious pumpkin seed snack for weeks. You can do it too!

On Halloween eve, I will light the carved pumpkins with candles and place them on the front porch as always, where they can be seen by passersby. Note: I do NOT place them outside a day or two in advance, as the excitable squirrels and festive masked racoons love to begin the holiday early!

I will purchase all the same wrapped candy I have given away in past years, this time to be placed in bowls outside the front door, where adventurous ghouls and critters can dine until the bowls are empty. Leftovers if any will be donated to the Groveland Food Shelf at Plymouth Congregational Church.

As a treat for courageous adults on the Halloween circuit, I'll place on the porch a generous self-serve wine bar and cheese platter with slices of rare roast beef, smoked salmon for the pescatarians, and a black bean salsa and dip for the vegans. Just kidding! But you deserve it!

If costumed gremlins do ring the bell, I will wave through the window glass, wearing my coyote skin headdress accentuated by a Dr. Fauci facemask!

Dear dear Dr. Fauci, a smart, decent public servant who worried about a coronavirus epidemic four years prior to its eruption, and worked hard to prepare our nation for it, now rewarded in ghoulish Trumptime by death threats on him and his family. He deserves all honor in our land. Other masks are welcome at the door as well, except the scariest of them all, the hydra-headed Trump/Pence mask, or worse, the Beelzebub McConnell mask, which would give me a heart attack on the spot!

Rethinking Rethinking Thanksgiving
(November 2020)

Thanksgiving was a revered holiday when I was a boy. The family piled into Dad's dusty Plymouth for the interminable thirty-mile trip From DePere to Appleton, Wisconsin. There we were greeted by my mother's family who enfolded us into a kitchen fragrant with turkey and stuffing.

Today the Thanksgiving holiday is under assault, and with reason. I remember in 1970 when Native American activists renamed it a National Day of Mourning. I understand. Listening to the voices of native individuals, tribes and their painful histories, in 1970 I founded one of the first college courses in the country in Native American Literature and taught it for 20 years. Nothing taught me as much as the stories from Native America I was not taught in school, the layers of history around us and under our feet filled with information about how to live appropriately on this land.

These two views of Thanksgiving opened a deep rift in my progressive Congregational church this year, where we debated the fate of a gloriously and laboriously embroidered tapestry of the Thanksgiving feast. After a year of listening to native voices and historians, discernment and spirited debate, the church membership voted nearly two to one to "rest" the tapestry out of sight. The majority believed that if certain imagery offended even a few, how could the church meet our obligation as an "open and affirming congregation?"

I voted with the majority but in fact my feet were firmly rooted on both sides of the divide.

I have always seen the story of Thanksgiving as aspirational, and still do, an expression of Martin Luther King's dream of racial harmony described in his iconic 1963 speech on the 100th anniversary of the Emancipation Proclamation. But it is worth remembering that King's speech opened not with a dream but with a nightmare catalogue of historical injustice. "We have come here today to dramatize a shameful condition," King thundered. His dream of harmony can only be realized after defeating the forces of shameful oppression and erasure.

Attacking that oppression, Abraham Lincoln fought the Civil War. Pursuing that dream, he established Thanksgiving as a national holiday, answering the entreaty of Sarah Josepha Hale whose idea had been refused by four previous presidents. In the midst of a bitter civil war, Thanksgiving became a necessary though hardly sufficient image of foundational amity.

That aspirational image still holds me, as Martin Luther King's dream holds me. Not as a balkanization of the racial and historical subsets of our nation, but as a revelation of its promise of harmony, mutual care and shared abundance. For the political world is not static.

The history of the suppression of America's native populations is gruesome from 1492 to essentially the Roosevelt administration, when positive political change finally began. That change has been slow but dramatic, spurred by political Native takeovers of Alcatraz island and Wounded Knee; marches on the Menominee reservation to reclaim control of their reservation; appointment of knowledgeable and sympathetic administrators at the Bureau of Indian Affairs; the opening of the nation's gambling loophole allowing tribally-owned casinos to flourish into the financial "New Buffalo" that brings not only jobs but political and economic clout to tribal nations; the rise of native lawyers schooled in treaty law and of courts willing to look at treaty facts, including the Boldt and Murphy decisions asserting tribal hunting and fishing rights that had been usurped by states and local governments for a century.

Many problems remain for native peoples in this country, but also many opportunities. The University of Minnesota founded the first Native American Studies program in 1969, overseen by a series of astute native Ph.D.'s, complimented today by 32 colleges run by native nations around the country. The Dakotah nation persists in its legitimate claim to the Black Hills, their treaty abrogated by the US government but never acceded to by the tribes in spite of a monetary settlement forced upon it. Meanwhile the largest ranch in the Black Hills was recently purchased and reclaimed by the tribes, with the help of a substantial gift from the Shakopee Mdewakanton band, a beginning. And at the ballot box, the heavy turnout by native voters helped deny a second term to an overtly unsympathetic President.

"Thanksgiving?" Or a "National Day of Mourning?" I prefer, and believe we can all still prefer, feasting together, all the rainbow colors and traditions of our nation at the table. That ideal is a distance from realization, but more than a dream.

The Third Squirrled War

(January 2021)

What a great idea, I said, as Susan came home with the latest pandemic winter gear, a Breeo "smokeless" fire pit. We tried it and it works! The idea is, invite friends to our back yard, 2 x 2 like Noah's ark, for an hour of warm, pandemic-distanced outdoor conversation, lubricated by house Hot Buttered Rum (it's hot and you'll like it).

But before invitations floated out over the smokeless flames, Susan thought she should warm up the yard. So she imported nine free-range balsam trees which she staked around the brick patio forming a sort of outdoor living room to shelter conversation. Another great idea. Go for it! What could go wrong?

Well… To set up the shelterbelt necessitated she move the bird feeder far enough away from the branches of the new trees but not too close to existing trees from either of which our resident squirrel acrobats could easily leap and savage the food she lays out for her beloved birds— mom and dad cardinal and prince and princess finch (gold and house) who have cast their lots with the missus to stay the winter and dine on her largess while she basks in visits of their smooth and elegant profiles.

Having been through The Tyranny of the Squirrels twice before, she was very strategic moving the feeder, its arms suspending her trays of goodies, seeking the one remaining backyard spot where she thought the squirrels could not succeed in their leaping thievery. You know the rest of the story.

As I write this on Saturday morning, Dec 12, 2020, Susan is alternately banging on the kitchen windows and loudly cursing the squirrels through the double-paned glass. Outside a squirrel perches, I must say cute as a cuddly stuffed animal all fluffed up in his thick winter coat, tail wrapped like a comforter. A good listener, he entertained Susan's muffled imprecations for several minutes before deciding which arm of the feeder he would ravage next.

So now I spend my winter days with an extremely intelligent woman in daily combat with equally intelligent gray squirrels, she banging on and shouting at the window while scheming further defenses, they playing along between leaps for lunch. Hardly defeated, she has a carful of confounding devices to try, though the outcome is fairly certain.

We had high hopes for peace this holiday season. The Angry Chicken inhabiting the White House for four long years had his Reign of Frenzy ended by the voters and the laws of the United States, the Army eager to move him out if necessary. The first of several Coronavirus vaccines was approved, others hot on its heels. Kudos to the scientists, manufacturers, supply chains, public officials, plus our son-in-law who worked 12-hour days from March to Thanksgiving without a day off managing vaccine trials, bringing hope for relief to the human population. Not that we humans deserve it, having allowed far too many Angry Chickens to seize countries by their crooked beaks. But at least our nation's nightmare is ending as petulant post-election lawsuits have been slapped away by judges bleary-eyed over the blizzard of fact-free chicanery.

Now Hannukah and Christmas and New Year's Day and Inauguration Day can be joyful again, our backyard compromise a small price to pay. Let the squirrels have their portion, and the birds theirs, and the trees theirs, and the people theirs, something God and Charles Darwin and Edward O. Wilson intended three billion years ago called the balance of nature. Looked at this way, the squirrels frisking around the backyard oak belong in the neighborhood as much as do we and the oak. And if attention is paid, the squirrels' remarkable acrobatics on the high wires of branches are worthy of admiration. As for the birds, they are the souls of our ancestors, their daily visits a comfort to our spirits.

With Winter cold late but finally closing in, the sun scratching the southern horizon as it arcs through short Solstice days, a warm Christmas truce is in force at the Urban Coyote household. Backyard fire lit, warm and smokeless, old friends slowly troop over, two by two, to remind us what the season is about, and tell their hopes and dreams for the days and decades ahead. We and the squirrels and the birds take it all in, listening together.

❧

Braiding "Braiding Sweetgrass"
(February 2021)

One of the joys of writing this column for the neighborhood newspaper is that the editor allows me to braid disparate strands – family, neighborhood, city, state, country, planet, state of mind – into these monthly Urban Coyote wanderings you hold in your hands. Pulling a column together feels a bit like braiding strands of sweetgrass into a fragrant portrait of life in our community. Strands, for example, of…

Dawn on Christmas day, swimming in Cedar Lake, walking in Lakewood cemetery, tennis in Kenwood park, attending the Honor The Earth powwow, watching birds at feeders and in migration, delighting at Halloween, inviting the neighborhood turkey to Thanksgiving dinner, a fiftieth wedding anniversary, city, state and national politics, the world view of Native America, the region's racist past and present struggle, meditating on it all while painting spindles, rooted in a remarkable "unintentional community" called neighborhood.

Yet today, January, 2021, we feel insecure. Insecure not primarily because of a spike in crime, though real, due mostly to Pandemic fallout, but because most of us, myself included, have failed at fully braiding our lives into the needs, wants and desires of other communities, including plant and animal communities other than our own hubristically self-proclaimed *homo sapiens sapiens.*

Sapiens squared? Give me a break! The brilliant bur oak in my backyard has outlived five generations of *sapiens sapiens* resident in this house since 1902 and will outlive this pandemic-humbled generation many times over again.

Kurt Vonnegut, Jr. saw through the smokescreen created by our "big brains" in the novels *Cat's Cradle* and *Galapagos.* In the first a scientist invents a compound, Ice Nine, that rearranges molecules of liquids into crystalline form. If accidentally dropped into a lake, not to mention the Great Lakes or an ocean, water would turn crystalline and all life would immediately end. And yet it was invented "because we can." In *Galapagos*, civilization has simply exhausted itself playing in its sandbox of wars, weapons, financial collapses and pandemics. Out of options, a few descendants survive on the remotest island of the Galapagos. The rest is all Charles Darwin.

Could there be another way? In *Braiding Sweetgrass: Indigenous Wisdom, Scientific Knowledge, and the Teachings of Plants*, Robin Wall Kimmerer shows us there is. A decorated Ph.D. botanist, professor of environmental science, and enrolled member of the Citizen Potawatomi Nation, Dr. Kimmerer eloquently weaves disparate strands of ancient tribal and modern scientific knowledge into a strategy for the return of ecological balance, healing not only our planetary home but our alienated human communities.

How can we become indigenous to a place? How can we live by the precepts of The Honorable Harvest: taking only what is given, using it well, offering gratitude for the gift, and reciprocating the gift? Will we learn to speak the "grammar of animacy," eliminating the distancing pronoun "it," instead recognizing the landscape around us as a community of relatives breathing and alive? Will we recognize "the tree people" as solid citizens of our neighborhoods who share our biological mantra, "we breathe, you breathe?"

"A great longing is upon us," Kimmerer writes, "to live in a world made of gifts." The gift her book gently teaches is to acknowledge the gifts Mother Earth has already arrayed around us, not as abstract "nature" but as co-equals in friendship and service. They breathe, we breathe.

The book has become a breakaway word-of-mouth bestseller since arriving over-the-transom at Milkweed Editions in Minneapolis, first published in 2013. According to the *New York Times Book Review,* by 2020 over 500,000 copies are in print in nine different languages. Like her beloved mosses, trees and sweetgrass, her audience quietly and persistently grows, now more than a million copies in nineteen languages as I write this column in the spring of 2021.

Will we be able to weave our local and planetary neighbors into the stories Kimmerer tells, and do so in time? She writes, *"We have braided a sweetgrass community, awakening for each other the knowing that we are not alone. The strength of that community has the power to activate change, and our collective rhizomes are spreading."* I feel the tickle of those rhizomes in my fingetips as I write.

Forgetting
(Spring 2021)

At a recent gathering of the extended family, all adults vaccinated, grandson Oliver Lenfestey, age five, showed off his marvelous magic skills. Before the final evening potluck he invited all to a magic show. Tickets, issued with his Mom's help, were little origami cups filled with popcorn. At the appointed hour, the curtain (a bath towel) dropped from the door before the assembled throng, revealing THE MAGICIAN!

His first trick succeeded masterfully. "Pick a card, any card. Queen of Hearts? OK, Place it back in deck." Shuffle, shuffle, cut, shuffle, cut, cut. Then the magician pulled a single card from the deck. "Queen of Hearts!" Cheers and claps all around!

Oliver was so excited, the response so appreciative, he developed a second magic trick *ON THE SPOT!* It went like this. "OK, Pick a card, any card. *Three of clubs.* OK, Show it to me and everybody. OK, now put it back in the deck. Now…, I am going to work *really really really* hard… *to forget it!*" Eyes scrunch, body spins, voice groans, hands pull at hair, more spinning. Then he jumped up… *"King of Diamonds!!!"*

And just like that, the genius of the child magician opened the door to wisdom on the calamitous year 2020-21 falling away behind us, what all of us can do. Work really really hard to turn a three of clubs into a King of Diamonds. By forgetting.

As vaccinations rapidly spread, the pandemic? Forget it.

As the pathetic Loser-in-Chief bumbles away from Twitter and the White House along with his deluded followers and insurrectionists, forget them.

The calamitous burning and looting of Lake Street, forget it.

The homeless encampments in Powderhorn and Kenwood Parks and along Lagoon, forget them.

The Chauvin trial coming to a close, let the justice system do its work.

Minneapolis and St Paul's record year for crime and homicides, and the flood of illegal guns on the streets, and the thoughtless "defund the police" mantra, forget them all for now.

And forget the idea of moving away to Arizona, with more than 144 days above 100 degrees Fahrenheit last year, more than 53 above 110 F, and climbing.

Ditto low tax, deeply racist Florida, the unforgiving ocean relentlessly eating away at its edges.

Ditto any other city and state. You think only we have race and class and climate problems! Forgetabouddit! Instead, stay and deal!

As scholar-philosopher Lewis Hyde considers in his latest path-breaking book, *A Primer on Forgetting: Getting Past the Past*, published in 2019, "We live in a culture that prizes memory – how much we can store, the quality of what's preserved, how we might better document and retain the moments of our life while fighting off the nightmare of losing all that we have experienced. But what if forgetfulness were seen not as something to fear – be it in the form of illness or simple absentmindedness – but rather as a blessing, a balm, a path to peace and rebirth?"

Peace and rebirth. Remember those? There will be time soon enough, as history and Lewis Hyde also remind us, for a "Truth and Reparations Commission" of our own design, much difficult work ahead to enfold so many neighbors once excluded.

But for now, as Mother Earth continues her voyage around the sun oblivious to the wandering ways of her human inhabitants, for right now... Bless the trees, they are budding! Great halos of buds! Angelic Afros of buds! Queen of Hearts and King of Diamonds and Ace of Spades buds! Pick a bud, any bud. And rejoice!

About the Author

James P. Lenfestey helped found the Hill and Lake Press, a community newspaper, in which most of these columns first appeared. After a career in academia, marketing communications, and journalism, on the editorial board of the *Star Tribune*, where he won several Page One awards for excellence, since 2000 Lenfestey has published a previous collection of Urban Coyote essays, seven collections of poems, edited three poetry anthologies, and co-edited *Robert Bly in This World* (University of Minnesota Press). His *haibun* memoir, *Seeking the Cave: A Pilgrimage to Cold Mountain*, was a finalist for the 2014 Minnesota Book Award. His sixth poetry collection, *A Marriage Book: 50 Years of Poems from a Marriage*, was a finalist for two 2017 Midwest book awards. In 2020 he received the Kay Sexton Award for significant contributions to the Minnesota literary community. For fifteen years he chaired the Literary Witnesses poetry program in Minneapolis and led a summer poetry series on Mackinac Island, Michigan. He lives in Minneapolis' Lowry Hill neighborhood with his wife, the political activist Susan Lenfestey. They have four children and eight grandchildren.